Some Serious Comments about the
Saga of a Fat Cat

Cute, and oh so true! I have the scars to prove it. Giggle...
cats are awesome, and you've offered some very helpful
advice here. Good job.
Annabel Sheila, writer, Newfoundland, Canada

Delightful, Stan. Love and peace to you,
Regis Auffray, writer, Peace River, AB, Canada

Oh my, a fat cat for dinner sounds wonderful...
Edd Matlack, writer, Landisville, NJ, USA

Hi Stan, Yep, it's the man's pride! LOL This sounds like
my mother's cat... he thinks he's from Somalia...
hahahaha...
The Bear Paw, writer, Ladysmith, WI, USA

Ha Ha Ha this brightened my day. Love it.
George Carroll, writer, NY, USA

CATS & DOGS
~~~and a~~~
Pig
~?~

by
Stan I.S. Law

Copyright © 2000, eBook 2010 by Stanislaw Kapuscinski
KINDLE EDITION 2011 reedited 2020
ISBN 978-1-987864-53-3
Published by INHOUSEPRESS

All rights reserved. No part of this publication may be
reproduced or transmitted in any form or by any means
electronic, mechanical, photocopying, recording or otherwise,
without the prior written permission of the publisher.
This book is a work of fiction. Names, characters, titles, places
and incidents are either the products of the author's imagination
or are used fictitiously.

Anthology of Verse
and
Short Stories

Our Park

My Cat is Fat

The Ark

I am a Fat Cat

Just my Luck

I am still a Fat Cat

The Broohos

Sphinx

Two of a Kind

Sharing

Dreamax

Bad Apple

To Sleep or not to Sleep

The Good Witch and the Warlock

Confirmation

Pig ?

These short stories are dedicated to:

Bartek
and Kaytek
and Maniusia
and Pimpah
and Maytek
and all their and my canine and feline friends.
Without them these tales would not have happened.

Our Park

"**Wuff!**" **I said politely.** One is expected to act in a civil manner in the most beautiful Park in town. A sort of heaven, really. Or as close to one as we are likely to get while still here. Here and now, that is. Many cites have beautiful parks, but the Mount Royal sets Montreal in a class of it's own. They say that from the top you can actually see heaven. Or the USA, or something.

She was a really beautiful bitch. Golden retriever, just like me, only she was pure gold. And those eyes! She turned them away the moment she saw me, but in that single instant I knew that fate brought us together for a purpose. Things like this only happen once in a blue moon. And we are not allowed to walk the Mountain during the night. Figure....

"Wuff-woof!" I repeated adding a hint of Westmout accent. I didn't want to be pushy, but, well, I already told you. The blue moon and all that. I had to take my chances.

And then, as George, my lord and master, attempted to change the retractable leash from one hand to another, with a single leap I managed to disappear into the bushes. George run after me, but, let's face it, he had no chance. I knew he'd feel guilty about inadvertently granting me my freedom. Strictly against the law. Human law. Arff, to the human law. I wasn't going to do anyone any harm. I've been around.

Anyway, it worked. Pretending that she was helping George to look for me the almond-eyed beauty took after me. In no time at all we were half-a-mile away, sitting almost side by side, on a flat piece of rock. She pretended that she'd found herself next to me quite by accident. I gave her the once... maybe the-twice-over. Then I rose elegantly from my haunches and strolled to the nearest tree. I managed to squeeze out a few drops. For a moment she ignored me. Then, looking away, she followed my footsteps. When I first got a whiff of her scent, my head spun. This was heaven all right.

"We really should go back, you know," she said at last.

"What's your name?" I countered.

Her long eyelashes once again trembled in the shimmering light, then lowered over her eyes as though examining her toes. I'd swear her nails have been manicured. "I am called Brandy," she wooffed hardly above a whisper. She was so shy it came out as Blantee.

To George it would sound like just another "bwuff", but to me it was the sweetest sound I've heard since George said "it's stake-time!"

But that wasn't really the point. Fate has a way of bringing together what was meant to be together.

"I am Cognac!" I said proudly giving my tail a swashbuckling swing.

"That's not funny," she said.

"Really!" I assured her displaying my collar. "Cognac as in Grand Champagne."

"I'm just... Brandy," she yelped softly. She sounded crestfallen.

"It's the most beautiful name I've ever heard!" I assured her.

"Really?" This was closer to a plaintive howl.

Dames are all the same. You throw them a bit of flattery and they lap it up. I? I need a good-sized bone before I'll wag my tail. When I wasn't picking up dames, that is. But she was beautiful. I mean, really.

"Really?"

Cripes! I've spent so much time with George lately I clean forgot that we—my species—could read each other's thoughts. She must have tuned in on my subliminal stream. There is another great advantage we have over George and his kind. We can't blush. Otherwise... Hey, how come I wasn't reading her thoughts?

"Race you to that hill!"

I was right. She'd read my thoughts before I actually said them and was off before I moved a leg. And what a runner she was! Why, she hardly touched the ground! She beat me by half a length. Of course, I would have won if it hadn't been for the retractable leash that didn't quite retract. Anyway, as she pulled up, I couldn't stop in time.

I bumped into her. Her silken fur rubbed against my neck. I swear it was an accident.

"Sorry!" I wooffed over my shoulder.

"Are you?"

This dame was hot. Blood rushed to my head, then drained to the tip of my tail. I felt weak. Like a teenager on his first date. Then I remembered what my father told me. "Son," he'd said. I was only a runt then. "Remember, when you think with your balls, you can't read anyone's thoughts!" Then as now, I panted in confusion. How come dames are so much cooler than us? We are supposed to be the strong-silent ones.

Finally I gathered enough courage to look at her again. This time she did not turn her eyes away. I thought I detected amusement in her gaze. Her tail was marking time like a metronome. I wondered if she knew about the problem we, machos, suffer from. Thinking-wise. I bet we could smell better, though. Right then, I would have bet my evening Alpo I could smell her excitement. I was still panting but was ready to propose another race—you know, just to try and beat her—when we both heard George talking to someone.

"It is she," Brandy wooffed softly. She licked her front paw. She wasn't even out of breath. Must have done a lot more running than I.

"She?"

"Jenny. My Lady. I bring her for runs every Sunday. She's quite good."

"You mean you run together every week?"

"Sometimes also in the evening. Mount Royal is really beautiful around sunset."

"Every week...? My mind was working overtime. If Brandy and what's-her-name come here every Sunday, all

I had to do was to make George take up jogging and I'll have it made. Holy Canine! To meet Brandy every week...

"It would be nice, wouldn't it," she threw over her shoulder.

I've done it again. She was reading me like an open book. Then I swallowed hard and took the bull by the horns. Or something like that.

"Would you consider..."

"Duck!" she let out a silent yelp as she leapt behind the bushes. I heard her. I heard her silent yelp!

I've never seen a duck but I ducked. George just never went hunting. Before I had a chance to think I followed her like an obedient puppy. That was not the way it was supposed to unfold. I was supposed to be the one giving orders. On the other hand, walking behind her I could smell her tail. I'm not stupid!

One whiff and I forgave her. For having faster reactions, I mean.

On the pathway winding its way through the thick bushy undergrowth, a couple emerged chatting nineteen-to-a-dozen. You've guessed it. George was huffing and puffing, doing his best to keep up with Jenny, who was prancing like a ten-year-old. Brandy was right. Jenny must have been running every week. She was slim, sun-kissed and, for a human, her hair was quite beautiful. It matched Brandy's only it was longer, of course. They didn't seem that worried about the two of us taking off. For a moment, I actually felt hurt. George should have worried about me. I could have gotten lost, or something. I never would, of course, but he should have worried anyway.

"How do you like her?" Brandy was at my side.

"Jenny? She's all right."

"I think she's beautiful."

Not half as beautiful as you… It was too late. She'd read me again.

"George is damn good looking," I countered trying to cover my embarrassment. And anyway, he was my George, and when I didn't make life hell for him, I liked him a lot. I mean he was my best friend.

"He really goes for Jenny," Brandy didn't say it, she just thought it aloud. That's a different kind of thinking. It's thinking with emotions. Such thoughts I could read anytime. Hormones notwithstanding.

And then it struck me.

George and I have been walking the Mount Royal on Sundays since early April. He didn't run, of course, not my dear George. Don't get me wrong. He isn't fat or anything, but if he were to shed some twenty pounds, it wouldn't hurt him either. And now that I think about it, I could swear that I had seen someone very much like Brandy before, only from a distance. They'd jogged past us… The problem is that seeing is not the same as smelling. Try it.

Brandy was busy grooming her legs, her ears and whatever it is that girls groom in the park. I knew she was listening. I am a quick study and she'd listened in to my thoughts before.

"I thought it would do George some good if they met," she said meekly. "He could loose a pound or two."

"He's just fine the way he is," I don't like being manipulated.

"B-but… but…"

Brandy stretched on the grass, all fours up, scratching her back. What could a fellow do? She was the most gorgeous bitch I've ever seen. Who cares if George falls for Jenny or the other way round, as long as they start jogging together. It wouldn't do me any harm either. And what if it was Brandy who thought of it first? So she was beautiful *and* smart.

Well, I was stronger.

And so was George.

George and I could take care of Brandy and Jenny in any Park. Even on the Mount Royal, after dark. It may be illegal, but... when the moon is blue...

"Cognac!" she was looking at me with those fantastic eyes. "You've been dreaming again." Then she looked behind her. "They went that way," she said. "Shouldn't we follow them?"

"Of course!" I took over immediately. After all, someone had to look after George. And Jenny, of course. Something told me that Brandy would be pretty good at looking after herself.

"This way," I said. I was myself again. She followed two paces behind me.

They were sitting on the grassy slope overlooking Pine Avenue. George was still talking; Jenny was still looking good, her sparkling eyes competing with the shimmering light filtering between the leaves. She really did have beautiful hair. Like a bunch of ripe chestnuts caught in early morning sunshine. Like Brandy's.

"Have you noticed," Brandy sounded coy, "that our car is parked just behind yours?"

"The world is full of coincidences," I assured her gravely. I had no idea what Jenny's car looked like.

"It certainly is," Brandy agreed. But she couldn't hide the grin that parted her beautiful jaws. And her tail was again working overtime.

"Ah, there you are!"

At long last they both noticed us. We've been sitting behind them stretching our bones for quite a while. Jenny continued to smile as though sharing some secret thought with Brandy. George got up and pulled Jenny up.

"See you next Sunday, then," he said, "if you promise to take it easy. I really haven't jogged for years," he added.

"And then some..." I detected Brandy's emotive thought as she glanced at my George. I gave her a dirty look but she ignored me. She was now preoccupied with Jenny. Bitches are like that. They stick together. Look after each other. Or... just then I caught Brandy's eye. Would you believe? She was laughing at me! Her tongue hanging out like there was no tomorrow....

Then Jenny shook George's hand and we all made for our respective cars.

As Brandy jumped into the back of Jenny's Pontiac, I just detected her emotive thought, this time directed at Jenny. "I think we got them, don't you?" she said silently.

Jenny appeared to understand Brandy quite clearly. "We most certainly have," she replied, hardly above a whisper. "We most certainly have." And she stuck her own tongue at Brandy. Would you believe it?

I had no idea what the two girls were talking about, but somehow I began looking forward to next Sunday with renewed interest.

***

My Cat is Fat

*Saga of a Fat Cat
Part One*

My cat is fat. He swallowed a rat.
He also eats too much for dinner.
If he was a she,
a lot more like me,
He would be both, cuter and thinner.

We went to a vet, a doc I'd just met.
He promised to make my cat leaner.
To cut off his—you know…
(that stuff down, below).
He said cat would keep his demeanor.

I really can't blame him; he's really so macho.
My dear pet—not the doc I'd just met.
My cat did a flip,
Turned at the hip.
And… the jet got the vet soaking wet.

***

The Ark

To tell you the truth, he could have said something. I mean to us—personally. Or at least mentioned it. Or told Bart about it. After all these years, that's the least he could have done. We've been guarding his place for as long as I can remember. Days, nights, it made no difference to us. And that goes for all of us: Sue, my brothers, Yin and Yang, and my baby sister, Babe. Not that Babe is much good at warding off the jackals or hyenas from the chickens, the ducks and the rest of the livestock, but she does her best. Sue, my mother, kept vigil over the household long before my brothers and I took over. Bart, my dad, is too old now, of course, but he's given Noah the best years of his life. And he'd served Lamech, Noah's father, before him. Dad doesn't do anything much any more. He just follows us with his eyes—when he's awake, that is. Which is not often.

Now, since Noah got this crazy idea, we aren't even sure he'll take us all with him. Especially dad. I think that after so many years.... he should. Dad's earned his keep. And the rest of us, well, we're all pretty useful. We look after him as much as he looks after us. Not like Purr and Whiskers who just lay about all the time. They wrap themselves into a sort of large seashell as if they were trying to swallow their own tails, and wait for the sun to set behind the horizon. But, somehow, they're both first when there's some food around. They could stay behind, as far as I am concerned. The canine members of the family should come first. Would Noah leave any of us behind?

"Pairs," he'd said. "Just pairs. There simply isn't room for more than one pair of every kind." He keeps repeating this round and round as if he'd heard it from the Big Dog in the sky or something.

No one ever questions what Noah says. He's the boss. I wonder what he's going to do with all the bugs. With the fleas and other bugs that bug me. Just pairs? I wish....

I can't really blame old Noah. He just woke up one day with this idea that it's going to rain. And he doesn't mean a shower or two, such as we get during the rainy season. Forty days and forty nights, he said. I mean really rain. Cats and dogs. No offence. But he talks as though the sky is about to come down and drown us all in a flood like you've never seen.

Well, I too have visions. I dream of juicy chunks of meat, of nice, plump rabbits, of occasional slices of what they're having for dinner. But rain? Give me a break. What's wrong with a bit of rain? At least that would keep the thieves away. No wonder nobody believes him. And now, with all this construction, it only gives Yin, Yang, and me extra work. And Babe, of course. We have to keep all the gaping peasants off the property. They just sit around and laugh.

"So where's this deluge you keep telling us about, Noah?"

Noah just looks sadly away.

They laugh and laugh. Those peasants are not very nice. And given half a chance, they would steal, I'm sure they would. There is a lot of valuable timber lying about. And Noah's storing dry food and other supplies, too. Dry!

That's a joke. According to him everything will be pretty wet, pretty soon. As a matter of fact, the Ark is only half-built and the sky is already getting darker day by day. Some days we get no more than an hour or two of sunshine. Not much fun.

Maybe the old man is onto something, somehow.

It's getting dark again, but I think it's already evening. Must be. Shem is laying the fire. Shem is a useful sort of a guy. He's not very bright, but works hard. Frankly, I don't think much of Noah's sons. They work, they help him, but they only do it because they're scared that their father is right and that they're really going to get good and wet.

Now, Ham is a different story. He's cool to the point of indifference. He doesn't think, he calculates. He is dark, swarthy, like his thoughts. He's no match for Shem physically, but he sure knows how to calculate the length of timber to fit the ribs of the ark. I don't think Noah would do well without him.

And then there is Japheth. He's fair, really handsome, almost like a girl. If you ask me, he's all-emotions. He can make a mountain out of a molehill any day. On the other hand, he's kinder to us than all of them put together. He is the one who remembers to make sure Bart always gets his share, even if he's late for dinner. I mean dad, not Japheth, although he's late, too, sometimes. Probably composing some songs by the river. I think he's a poet.

But it's Noah who keeps us all together. If Shem, Ham and Japheth are sort of muscle, brain and heart of the family, Noah is the guide. There is a strange peace about him. No matter how the peasants pull his leg, about the ark, I mean, he never loses his cool. He is a very wise man. Wise, calm, and old. He keeps his family together like Bart keeps us together.

And then there's Na'amah, the Beautiful, Noah's wife. She embodies all Noah's traits without ever showing them off in any way. Bart says she's like Noah's soul, like his subconscious, but I don't really know what that means. Dad tells me that in humans, subconscious is like instinct with us, dogs. We just know things even if we don't quite know how we know. A sort of sixth sense. The other five I understand. Senses, I mean.

So that's our family. There are also the three wives of the three sons, but there is little I can tell you about them. They sort of cook and giggle and that's about all.

Last week we had the topping off ceremony. That's when the roof was closed over our heads. And not a moment too soon. The rain showers were getting longer, and cooler. My brothers and I were happy there was a large place indoors we could dry out in. Soon Noah will start collecting the pairs.

The word 'pairs' makes me shiver. How can he talk about pairs when there is dad and mom and Babe and Yin and Yang? I'll tell you one thing. If Noah doesn't take all of us, then I am not going. Even if he does choose me. But I'm not a pair. I guess he'll have to choose a bitch from one of the other families. I could do it myself but, well, I was just too busy. What, with the construction and all. And now am I going to be punished for working so hard? It just doesn't sound like Noah. On the other hand, he does keep repeating this 'pairs' business. I'm telling you, it makes me shiver. I suppose I'll stay and die with my parents. Of course they're a pair, but they're too old to have pups. Not at their age. Anyway, they gave me life, they will take it. Together. Like it should be. I hope the Great Dog in the sky will give me strength.

I'll miss them. I suppose, I'll miss Na'amah most. She's so beautiful. No wonder they call her The Beautiful. And she's so kind. She seems to know, in advance, what Noah wants—like she's reading his mind. Like Whiskers. Or Purr, for that matter. I can see the way Noah looks at her. When he sees her, there are stars in his eyes.... As for me, there is just one thing that annoys me about her. You've guessed it—Purr and Whiskers. When the two of them, yes, a pair, are not asleep, they keep rubbing their heads and ears or bodies or whatever it is that cats rub, against Na'amah's legs. Or they jump on her lap and just stay there. As if they owned her. She's too kind, of course, to throw them off. I would. Not that I have a lap, exactly, but you know what I mean. They're lazy. I told them that once... sort of.

"Have you seen any mice lately?" Purr asked, licking his foot.

"Or rats?" Whiskers added.

"Or *any* rodents?" they asked together.

I just looked at them and thought, "I've never seen you catch anything. Lazy cats, you probably don't know how to hunt, anyway."

"We do it at night, when you're snoring," Whisker purred.

"I don't snore, funny face," I barked. She'd read my thoughts. Cats have this weird habit of reading every one's thoughts. I hate that.

"Easy boy!" Purr hissed ever so gently. It's funny that. The bigger his tail gets, the softer he hisses. And at the same time his talons come out by about three inches.

"Birds have talons," Whiskers meowed. "I have claws. And anyway, they are not three inches."

She sounded as if she took the three-inch thing as a compliment.

"Aaah, forget it," I said, as softly as I could. "I've got work to do."

I'm the eldest brother. I had to offer an example of self-control. And anyway, by the time I swaggered off they both looked asleep. I hate cats.

The ark is finished and it's impressive as hell. I've never, I mean NEVER, seen anything that big. It looks like a mountain. At least thirty cubits high. Maybe taller. And three hundred cubits long and fifty cubits wide. That's like twenty houses stuck side by side along its length. Probably more. Or fifty tents. Really. I've never seen anything.... I've already told you that. Nobody has ever seen anything that big. Nobody. It takes forever to run from one end to the other. Babe can't even make it; she has to stop and walk.

The storage spaces are full of food and the first pairs have begun to arrive. Two camels and two monkeys turned up one morning. The food Noah has is fine for them but what about the carnivores? What about them? What are they going to eat? After all, there will probably be lions and tigers, and pumas, and... Great Dog! I'm a carnivore, aren't I?

And then, suddenly, it hits me. Noah didn't pack any meat because no carnivores are going on board. I look around.

"On the other hand, cats eat meat too!" I whisper.

This cheers me up no end. As a matter of fact, if the water rises to our level, I'm a hell of a lot better swimmer than either Purr or Whiskers. I might even make it to some high ground and wait it out. The flood, I mean. I'm so sure about mom and dad. Distance swimming takes a lot out of you. How can Noah come up with these stupid rules? How can he?

You wouldn't believe how many pairs there are in the world. I imagine, thirty or forty? I don't go around counting pairs, you know. But there must be hundreds of them. More. I can't believe how many. Big and small. How on earth did Noah know how big the ark needed to be? When this all started, Noah stood on a large rock and gathered all of us around.

"...every living thing that is of flesh, two of every sort... they shall be male and female." That was the first time that this pair-business came up.

"...birds after their kind," he said. I bet Purr and

Whiskers loved that. I bet they'll give those birds a proper run-around.

"...and cattle after their kind, and every creeping thing of the ground after their kind, two of every sort... will keep them alive."

He must have been talking about those fleas I told you about. Two of every sort, my foot. Just how many sorts of fleas are there, anyway? And all the other bugs crawling. I don't mind telling you, it gives me the creeps just thinking about them! They bite, for crying out loud!

That's about all he'd said before he made the calculations for the ark. The size I mean.

Hey! Maybe he isn't taking the lions and tigers and hyenas after all. Just cattle, birds and bugs. They wouldn't be too bad. But if that's true, then why three hundred cubits?

Something's fishy. Then it hits me right between my eyes. Of course! The carnivores will eat fish! Sometimes I'm so smart I surprise myself. With water all around us, we can fish all the time. I mean *they* can fish. Shem and Ham and Japheth and their wives. That's a lot of fish!

Noah must have worked it all out. He might have missed out on the pairs, but he's as sharp as the spikes we used in construction.

The pairs just keep coming. The queue's as long as the eye can see. For some reason, the carnivores aren't eating the herbivores, and even the omnivores are keeping their fangs to themselves. Noah must have thrown some sort of hex over them. Behave or stay behind, I suppose. That's a persuasive thought. This Noah, I tell you, is some sort of a guy. Whoever gets close to him, they become calm. I mean, immediately. Serene and kind. To each other, I mean, no matter how obnoxious they were the day before. That's really strange, because Noah's father, Lamech, was strong like Ham, but he was wild. He destroyed things. Noah is probably even stronger, but he builds things instead. Like the ark.

And what energy Noah has. Bart told me that Noah's six hundred years old, but he moves like a young man. Really. Bart knows a lot of things. Sometimes he gets up at night and just looks at the sky. I've heard people say that Bart howls at the moon. I know it isn't so. Bart told me once that he's invoking the power of Sirius, a bright star in the Dog Star something or rather. Constipation I think he called it. The most important star in the sky, he said.

"A day will come when the sun and Sirius will dry up the land, after the big water," he prophesied. Father does that. He sees the future. Not much of the present, but he's big on the future.

There isn't much to do anymore. The loading's going to take another day or two, and there's nothing left for the peasants to steal. We—Yin, Yang and Babe—are just lying around having some well-earned time off.

"You're wrong about this pair business," Babe says.

Girls always think they know everything.

"She's right," Whiskers pipes up. Of course, females always stick together. Even cats and dogs. On the other hand, cats know things dogs don't. That's because they can read your thoughts. But we can smell better.

I wag my tail. I'm listening. I've never hoped so much to be proven wrong. Even by a cat.

"When Boss spoke of pairs, he also said that he'd take seven and seven of every clean beast, male and female, but only two, also male and female, of the unclean beasts. The same goes for the birds. I don't know what'll happen to the bugs, the crawlers, but frankly I don't care very much."

Seven and seven. Dad, Sue, Babe, Yin, Yang and me, that's . . . that's...

"Six, oh Great Mathematician," Whiskers purrs, with her usual condescending smile.

I've never been much good at math, but there's no need to be sarcastic. "No offense," she adds, even more softly. Maybe she isn't such a bad sort after all.

"See!" Babe jumps on my back.

"Get off!" She's so childish. Whenever Babe is happy she jumps on me when I least expect it.

"I told you, I told you," she chants dancing around.

So there's a chance that we might make it aboard. But there's still a problem. We aren't pairs. Apart from mom and dad, we're kin. Not that good for having pups.

Dad's been listening to all this from afar. I thought he was sleeping. His eyelids were so low, they looked like they were on his cheeks.

"Gather around," he rasps. His throat's gotten pretty rough from years of barking.

Somehow we all hear him. When Dad speaks, all listen. He is as smart as any dog in history. Some say he's as smart as Noah, but I think that's pushing it.

"Gather around and listen," dad repeats. "I'll tell you things you don't know. Even most humans don't know what I am going to tell you."

That does it. Even humans don't know? I'm happy

when I see Purr and Whiskers advance and lie down in front of Dad's nose. First row seats for those two. As always.

"Now listen closely, for these are great secrets I am going to tell you," Bart says, his voice gathering strength as he continues. He must have been a magnificent dog when he was younger.

"Not all things are as they seem..." he begins, and suddenly there's great silence all around. Even some birds fly close and gather on outcroppings of rocks. And then nature stands still. We all forget about the line of animals waiting close by. We forget about Noah and the ark and the flood. We listen.

"Things are not always what they appear to be," Bart repeats. My head feels funny and I feel nervous. It's like he's only talking to me. Perhaps he is. Maybe the others feel like it too. Bart has strange powers. He is our Noah, our guide.

"There are times, when we forget why we are here. We lose sight of the purpose of life. And, my children, there is purpose to everything. To every beast and cattle, to every bird that can fly, to everything that crawls under our feet. There is nothing that is and shouldn't be."

Bart looks around. His smile is as kind as Na'amah's. He is as peaceful as Noah himself.

"The essence in every one of us, is but one. There are no beasts or cattle or creepy-crawly things that are apart. Neither are there birds nor fish. There is only life that permeates every one of us and finds different forms of expression. But it is the single life, the single consciousness that permeates us all. Whiskers knows that. That is why she can read your thoughts."

"But why is it that I cannot read yours, Sir?"

Whiskers asks, nevertheless pleased at being singled out from all present. Neither my sister nor by brothers would dare to interrupt when Bart's speaking.

"Thoughts, little one, are not the essence of our being. They are generated by our intellect. At least thoughts that are already translated into words, into symbols of that of what we are thinking. I do not do that. I speak directly from my consciousness. From my heart, you might say. The words are only formed as they leave my mouth."

Whiskers nods satisfied.

"So you see, that in essence, Noah is not saving anyone. We are all present in each other. In each one of us."

"But the Ark?" I blurt out before I can stop myself.

"Aah, the ark, my boy. The ark is a symbol. A symbol of the very thing I am talking about. It is a state of consciousness in which we are all unified. In which we are all under the same roof, so to speak."

He looks at us with great patience. "And the flood, you might well ask? Well, yes, there will be a flood. At least, it very much looks like it. Noah is very clever in predicting the weather. When you're six hundred years old, you gather a great deal of experience in such matters."

"So there will be no..." The words escape Babe quite unwittingly.

"Yes, there will very likely be a great flood. And great many species will be in danger of drowning. But that would not explain why Noah wants seven of each of male and female, does it?" His ancient jaw drops releasing a little saliva on his paws. Dad's very old for a dog. Very old indeed.

Just then I look up and see that the animals in line

have slowed down. They aren't plodding forward to the ark. They're looking over at our little group. Are they trying to hear what Bart is saying? Who wouldn't? There's only one Noah among the humans, only one Bart among the rest of us.

"Seven, my children, symbolizes fullness, and fullness implies perfection. When you can neither add nor subtract anything, that state is a holy state. A state of Wholeness. Do you understand?"

All of us nod.

"But what about the unclean couples...?" this is Babe again. She is such a baby.

"The unclean couples are the imperfect conditions, or those that still need work to become perfect. Don't forget, there is nothing without a reason under the great Sirius. Nothing under the sky."

Suddenly, I feel tired. I fight it hard, but can't resist. I rest my head on my paws and my eyes close. Bart's last words, 'there is nothing without a reason', still run through in my head.

I see Noah standing on a hill. His silhouette shakes and then splits into four parts. One remains on the highest rock, the others look like his sons. One has no mind or emotions, just a big hunk of muscle. One looks like he's trying to understand something real difficult, his brow all furrowed. And the third looks kindly at the world around him; he's warm and friendly. The next moment Noah shrugs, and all three sons go back into his body. They're one again.

As I open my eyes, I see father looking at me.

"They are all one, my son. We are all of fourfold nature. There is our true consciousness. There is also the physical, emotional and the one controlled by our intellect.

But we are all one, in essence."

I nod knowingly, still not sure if I really understand. I'm not even sure how he knew what I was thinking. Everyone else is nodding too. They can't have had the same dream? That's impossible!

"We are all one," Bart repeats slowly, a smile playing about his jaws.

Slowly I'm beginning to understand what my father's been talking about. There's only one thing left to settle. Can I ask? I needed to know that if there really is going to be a flood, and if only pairs are allowed aboard the ark.

We've all been so absorbed in Bart's words that not one of us noticed that the long line of pairs has already disappeared into the body of the ark. Noah's sons are getting ready to raise the ramp. I guess we won't be invited to join them inside. Neither the clean nor the not so clean.

"The great flood will cleanse the earth, our lower nature, from misguided concepts. When it is over, we shall settle atop a mountain, and rejoice in the new earth. And the mountain's name shall be Ararat. It will be high above all plains. It shall give us all great perspective on the new life," Bart says scratching his ear.

But not for all of us, I think. And then Noah calls us.

"What is the matter with you all? Can't you see that we are ready to raise the ramp?"

"B-b-b-ut, the p-p-pairs...."

"What pairs, silly? You are family. Now come along. You've rested enough!"

Noah actually taking with the dog?

My jaw drops as I look at my father. I have a strange feeling that he knew all along. Maybe Sue also knew, she looks very calm. Perhaps we all get calmer as we grow older.

"You see, son, our thoughts are unclean. We need a good flood to wash them out," dad says from the corner of his mouth.

For the very first time I'm sure that I really understand his words. I understand what it means to be one, to be family. I run to the ark, happy for the first time in weeks. Great Dog! What a stupid mutt I was. I wasted so much time worrying about being left behind.

***

I Am a Fat Cat

Saga of a Fat Cat
Part Two

I am a fat cat. I swallowed a rat.
I also ate too much for dinner.
If I were a she,
I must agree,
I would be both, cuter and thinner.

We went to a vet, a doc she'd just met.
He promised to make her cat leaner.
To cut off my—you know…
(It's just the last straw!)
I would be still too fat, but meaner.

Don't ever toy with a tomcat's joy.
Not if you're a pirate from Somalia…
Don't be a fool,
remember the rule:
Don't even touch cat's regalia.

***

Just My Luck

I must say, it hurts like blazes. For an instant I was sure I was dying. Or dead. Almost. Only it hurts too much. Dead people don't hurt, do they? What son of a bitch would kick anyone in the kidneys? I blink a dozen times, stretch and then, for a while, I stop breathing all together. There is something very wrong. For crying out loud... I feel funny, funny peculiar, all over....

I glance behind me. The face that stares at me in the broken mirror a foot in front of my nose has whiskers, eyes with vertical irises and... and it stinks to high heaven. Now I know I'm dreaming. Reflections don't stink. Skinny, scrawny, godforsaken cats do. I close my eyes and decide to wake up. Dreams are fine, but not when they're embellished with excruciating pain along the spine. The bastard really let me have it. Me? He let the cat have it. An inch lower and...

According to the mirror there is hardly anything left of me an inch lower. If he kicked me a few inches lower, or higher for that matter, he would have missed me. He would have missed the cat.

What cat?

I have to cut down on bourbon. This dream is loosing its fascination, and the pain isn't getting any better. Why can't I dream that I'm a bird, or a fish, or something. Or even a man who kicked a lousy cat, instead of the other way round?

I glance again at the broken mirror behind me. I decide to stop drinking altogether. It must have been that last bourbon. The one-too-many. For some reason, whatever it is that is looking back at me is furry, has black and white patches all over, as though whoever had painted its hairy hide couldn't make up his mind. Its ears point up, the legs are too short, and get this, the tail, right, the *tail* is pointing straight up like a flagpole. When it moves my spine hurts like hell. That's right. Like the blazes.

"Meooowww...." escapes my parched lips. At least I think they are my lips. Either that or they belong to the patchy beast impersonating me.

The gaunt, spindly cat continues to stare at me with suspicion oozing out of its eyes. *Stupid dream.* I remember we went out, actually we sort of reeled out from the pub, propping each other up against the guardrails and the lampposts. I remember feeling almighty. I could do everything—except walk straight, that is. Neither could George nor Fred. There was also a bunch of other guys. We'd just won the rugby match against Gypsy Saracens. It was tough, vicious, you could say, but we won. By one single try. We couldn't even convert it, but it was enough.

Hell, my back hurts...

We had to celebrate. The last time the Gypsies made mincemeat out of us. They beat us by twenty-six points. Ah... sweet revenge. Now we are kings. We are Victors Ludorum. The Champs.

"Out of the way," George had shouted.

The stupid cat was stretching in the middle of the sidewalk. Didn't it know that the victors have the right of way? I gave it a little kick in the kidneys. Nothing much but I lost my balance. There was this screech of brakes and... and something hit me hard. Real hard. The s.o.b. must have been speeding. Some people....

Then things got sort of dark. My buddies hid behind a peculiar grey haze. They just weren't there any more. Good God! The lousy twerp hit me with his right bumper—threw me right in the air. Serves him right. He'd lost his side mirror. *I am not dying, am I? Not on the day of our victory? We aren't through celebrating!*

So where's this tunnel of light? The Pearly Gates? OK. The sulfurous flames...?

I glance at the broken side mirror. I am licking my side.

I AM LICKING MY HAIRY, BLEEDING, TANGLED FUR!

I am a cat. I am a black and white, otherwise nondescript, cat. At least nondescript to me, at first sight. No pedigree, no shiny, carefully brushed fur. I am not just a cat. I am an alley cat. That's as low as you can get. That's like being an unemployed Mexican in New York on an expired work permit.

I am a cat.

Either that, or I am about to wake up and beat the hell out of the guy who'd run me down. With my buddies I'll give him a proper going over. Only there are no buddies. I look around. Even that's painful. I am lying in a gutter half-filled with some stinking garbage. Some fellows are picking up another guy up some ten yards further down the curb. He looks in bad shape—sort of hanging all loose and limp. I can't believe my eyes.

Hey! You there! Careful! That's my....

The wailing ambulance takes what is left of the body.

...what's left of my body?

I MUST WAKE UP!!!

The grey haze lifts a bit....

I see my buddies reeling from one side to another. After a while they start singing. Don't they miss me, already? Sounds like a victory jingle. All I hear is "glory, glory alleluia... and his soul went marching on." Well, I don't know were he was marching, but I ain't going anywhere. It hurts too much. It hurts to retract my nails. Claws? The guys still sound drunk. I wonder why people drink so much. What do I care?

I lift my left leg and lick my stomach.

I must stop doing that!

The haze descends again. For some reason, the fate of the fellow who got run over is already a matter of quite unparalleled indifference. It is about then that it begins dawning on me that I am not going to wake up. For some reason, I am now a cat, and not one pampered by some dear old lady. I am an alley cat whom some yokel kicked in the kidneys and left for dead. Only I'm not dead. Probably something to do with nine lives.

The pain in my side is getting better. More tolerable. I try to get up. It's good to have four legs. On third attempt I make it. I have to find a hole somewhere where I can sleep it off. And then food, only that has to wait.

I must have dozed off. I dreamt I was a drunk. Then I got all hairy. When I come to, it is still dark. I feel I should flag a taxi, or report the accident to a cop or something. The next instant I stretch my spine. *Taxi?* Stretching takes all my attention. It also removes tension and it tingles all over. Nice. I chew out all the bugs in my fur. They itch.

How come I had no bugs when I was... what was his name?

What is my name?

Somehow being a cat no longer surprises me. My skin feels quite natural. I lick myself as clean as I can, and embark on a search for some chow. Ideally, I would love to be adopted. By anyone. But this has to wait. Then I feel a whiff of something familiar. It's coming from down the road. I've been there before. (*I'd never been there).* There's a restaurant. Slowly I make my way along the guardrail, making sure I could duck between the vertical rods at a moment's notice.

And then it strikes me. If I'd just become a cat, how come I'm not a cute little kitten? Aren't we all born little?

The smell is getting stronger. They must have just closed and cleaned up some garbage at the rear lane. I hate eating from a garbage can, but, well, you know, beggars can't be choosers, and right now I'm a first class, limping beggar.

Let me tell you, being a cat is no fun at all. Not an alley cat.

The stuff wasn't half-bad. Do you know, some

people eat just about half what's on their plate? Judging by the leftovers, the sizes of steaks they serve are enough for three men and about a dozen cats. I mean that. Soon I can't eat another bite.

I find a nice dark corner to sleep in, just behind the bin. The roof overhung would protect me in case it started raining. On the other hand, the rain would give me something to drink. I am thirsty, parched, but just too tired. I lick some water from a small puddle. My kidneys are beginning to hurt again. That son of a....

When I wake up, I decide to review the situation. It seems—indeed there is no other explanation—that when the car hit me, I'd entered the body of the cat I'd kicked. What I have to figure out is just in which life the cat is presently dwelling. If cats have nine lives, then I could have another eight to go.

For crying out loud, nine lives?

I don't like the idea at all. I wonder if one can escape one's Karma. Especially if one is a cat. Only I'm not really a cat. I am a sod of a rugby player in a cat's body. Funny, how I can still remember that?

I don't know how to test my theory. Then it comes to me. I walk to the middle of the road and just sit there. If a car runs me down, I'll be over and done with. I will probably be reborn as some sort of cute baby, to some cute-as-hell mommy. Of course, that's if I'm still a boy. It would be a lot less exciting, or perhaps even more so, if I were to be a girl. But never mind that. For now, I just have to sit there and get run over.

For half an hour that feels like a week not a single car comes by. Not one. How come that idiot got run over yesterday and I can't get even one lousy car to get near me? I decide to give it another ten winks, tops, and then look for some food. My mind wants to get on with it, by my body is screaming for food. When I'm hungry, my body I mean, I can't think straight. It seems that I am an eat-little-but-often type of a cat. I didn't know that alley cats have a choice of menu, but, surprisingly, there is an abundance of food everywhere. This body has a memory of its own. And what a nose! I can smell fish practically all around me.

Am I thinking like a cat?

I'm certainly smelling like one. Seriously, my olfactory sense is inhuman. If I were still the old me, I could have become a famous gourmet. Or a chef with a big white hat. Or a wine taster. Too late. I leave the street and make my way to my domain. The alley. It's amazing how quickly hunger catches up with you. One moment you're quite happy, and the moment you've just got to eat something. I think that's why cats sleep so much. It's to stop us from eating all the time. All right, most of the time.

How come I think like a cat?

I follow my nose. Up ahead there is food. There is also a big black monster of a tomcat gorging himself on some delicious looking fish that didn't care any more who ate it.

One swift kick in the kidneys and all that stuff could me mine! Although that Tom looks soooo attractive….

Ouch… it hurts to even think about it….

That restaurant is a gold mine. And then I stop. Something tells me that things aren't as they should be. I peek between my legs. I thought so. Nothing. I am a girl. My instinct tells me that girls should avoid big, fat tomcats. No matter how beautiful they are. As silently as I can, I change direction and jump on the fence. The pain nearly kills me. From this vantage point I can observe the glutton and make my way to the restaurant when he is good and done. It doesn't take that long. I know that once he'd gorged himself, he'd have to sleep it off. My time would come. Cat's can be pretty patient when need be.

I never was.

I am hearing echoes?

Ten minutes later my belly is full. I, too, decide to take things easy. After all, there is no hurry with this dying business, and living in the alley isn't as bad as some say. At the moment I have no idea who 'some' are, or were. Maybe even that big tomcat might prove to be nice....

In my sleep I'm run over. Really. I dream that I'd been run over by a car. I didn't die. I gathered the gooey stuff with my disjointed paws from all over the tarmac and sort of pushed it together into a general shape of a cat. When I regained my senses, I decided to find a different way to test my nine-lives theory.

For a while I sit and watch people. Humans. Some look vaguely familiar.

By the second day I forget why I wanted to find out about the whatever-it-was life hypothesis. Yet, for some reason, I hope the body I am in is in its last life. By the evening I take a quiet stroll, to maybe meet some company. And there he is. He looks young, maybe inexperienced, but we could run around together. He must belong somewhere. He looks clean, looked after. Maybe he would invite me in? Anyway, as I was saying, we could run around together for a bit. Nothing permanent. Just for fun. Like cats do. Well, alley cats. I point my tail straight up. I find that funny. It's fun being a cat.

I watch people some more…. They have no tails.

A group of street urchins are kicking a ball to each other. They look rough, but seem preoccupied with their game. They fill the space between the object of my admiration and myself. I sneak around until I have to cross a piece of open terrain. The rock hits me exactly in the same spot some bozo had kicked the other day. At least I think someone kicked me. Anyway, it hurts like hell. Surely, this time I will die. I have to. The pain is unadulterated agony. I only just manage to clear the corner of the building and slither down the stairs to the basement. There I crawl under a wooden door into some sort of storage shed.

The last thing I remember, before I blacked out, is an amazingly clear notion.

Two down, it said to me. *Seven to go.*

Just my luck, I thought. And then all things turned black, again.

***

Saga of a Fat Cat
Part Three
(I made my cat promise it's the last part)

I am the cat that swallowed a rat.
I'd also eaten too much dinner.
But you must agree
that I'm a real "He",
I can be both, macho and thinner.

Remember the vet, the guy she'd just met,
who'd promised to make me leaner?
He could suck out my fat,
get rid of the rat,
and I would be an all round winner!

Instead of the vet, guy I hardly met,
Put his hand where no one should reach!
I bit on his thumb
I bet it's still numb.
A lesson I was bound to teach.

***

So if you ever reach down,
(where you cannot see)
lose a finger or thumb, well…

don't ever blame me.
If you must go there, do it
when cat's still a kitten.
Even then, if you are wise,
you'll wear a thick mitten.

*****

I am Still a Fat Cat
(And there's a devil on my shoulder)

The Broohos

"**M**ommy?"

"Yes, dear?"

"Why do the two-things walk some ten gorks behind the four-things and pick up their brooh, and then continue as if nothing has happened."

Movement was important to Hia, hence two- and four-things. As for brooh, Hia has seen it on Mars. It was much smaller, and didn't smell so badly. Even from this distance.

"That's because the four-things do not digest everything they absorb. You cannot do that with solid matter, dear." Hea smiled at her daughter. "And the two and four things are called legs."

"But how on Mars did they train them to do it?"

"Not on Mars, darling. On… the two-things would call it on Ars."

"Ars? No, Mommy, that's not it. I think they call it Soil."

"No, soil is what brooh does. It soils," Mother said, all the time searching her memory for the name of the third planet from the sun. Then she nodded with satisfaction, "They call it Earth, like soil only, well, I just can't figure it out. Earth or Soil. It sounds like dirty earth."

"What do you expect? If all they are good for is

picking up brooh, then you can't expect them to speak properly. It sounds as though they got lots of words mixed up."

"You're right. That's why they keep saying things like 'you know', when nobody has any idea what they know."

"I know, it's contagious." Hie giggled—sparks effervescing from her like tiny fireworks—at her own play on words. "Have to look out for it."

"And don't call them Broohos," Hea added. "It's not nice. They only pickup the brooh to keep their planet clean."

There was a momentary silence as they both watched the two-things picking up brooh after one of the four-things. They appeared to hide it in a plastic bag, then carry it protectively in their hands.

"Anyway, their masters communicate at a higher level, dear. They only use sound when they want to attract the attention of, ah, of their Broohos. The two-things. Otherwise it's all-subliminal. Must say, they look quite admirable."

"Maybe we shouldn't call them Broohos, Mommy, but that's what they do, don't they? There must be other things they can do…"

"I think they also do other chores, like shopping for food." Mother scanned her memory. "And, I suspect, the four-things also use them to erect enclosures to protect them from vicissitudes of their unregulated climate."

Ham watched this exchange without sharing a thought. He just loved witnessing his wife and daughter crossing new ground. He and Hea have been together for seven Zodiacs and now, finally, a tiny part of them individualized itself from their union. Living proof that love is the ultimate creator. They would never be truly apart, but Hia will contribute yet another viewpoint to their experience of reality.

"I believe they refer to themselves as Men," he now put in.

"You're kidding. Their climate is unregulated?"

Hia, his daughter, ignored her father's interruption. What the little one had forgotten was that no climate is ever regulated. It is they, he and mother and Hia, who regulated themselves to be oblivious to all climates. Essentially, they were individualizations of the omnipresent Hu.

"Not only that. The Broohos, sorry, Men, continually pollute it to make it even worse. On the other hand, the four-things use them to perform all the utile tasks to enhance their lives. You know, like production of comestibles, shopping, cleaning, even to provide them with primitive means of transportation."

"Men," Ham put in again. "Men, and the four-things are called Canines."

"So they are not all that stupid, after all?" There was hope in Hia's tone of thoughts.

"Well, they can drive their gascars quite well, but there are plenty of smashups. Smelly things, though."

"Like brooh?"

"Well, perhaps not as bad…"

Mother managed to stifle a laugh. Hum didn't do so well, and moved a light-year away, not to interrupt the object lesson. This was the first trip on which they took their daughter to a different planet.

"They would be all right if it weren't for the fact that whenever the Canines leave them alone for a bit, they start arguing, robbing each other, even removing their Hu. I understand they also indulge in mass recycling exercises, without anyone benefiting from them."

"I heard. They call them wars. Is that why the Canines keep them always on a leash?" Hia nodded to herself. It looked like air rising and falling over a hot—and immediately cooling—surface.

"Funny sort of sport, this war business…" they heard dad's thought from afar.

"Not really sport, though they take those exercises quite seriously. When they use projectiles, they also call these pass-times armed conflicts, or military actions. The poor saps haven't learned yet that they can transfer their Hu from one person to another," Hea added. She was no longer enjoying this excursion.

"Nah, they're much too primitive for that," again dad put in, this time from much closer.

"Can Canines do it?" Hia wanted to know everything.

"They must, I suppose. I never saw them start a war. And they spend most of their time sleeping. I believe Hu travel is by far their favourite pastime."

"I thought they haggle over their territory."

"Some, but hardly over a few extra gorkos. Usually only to release inner tension, probably built up by living with the Broohos. I mean Men," she corrected herself looking if dad was around again. Not sensing his presence, she breathed a sigh of relief. Ham had so much more self-control then she. "It can't be easy."

"Pull up, here comes one."

The next instant they were hovering about a hundred gorkos above the ground. The day was clear, sunny, and if it weren't for the smell of gasoline and brooh, it would be perfect.

"Look, Mommy," Hia filled the sky with her smile.

"One Brooho pulled on a long leash by two Canines. I must say they've got them well trained."

"Man. One Man." Dad was back. "Actually I think the Canines only brooh here and there to make Man feel wanted. Sort of... indispensible?" Dad was always the quintessence of kindness. His wife, Hea, thought that that was why they were blessed with Hia.

"They really look after their servants. Must be a nice race. I wonder how soon they'll start Hu travel outside their own planet."

"I suspect they are very close. I heard one singing to the moon the other day. Quite lovely, actually…"

"Howling?" Hea asked.

"You're a romantic, aren't you?" Dad's memories went back a few long millennia.

"Well, it's only a few thousand years since I was doing the same thing looking at the Soil. I mean Earth."

"How time flies…"

Two Canines went by, waging their rear appendages, which, surely, expressed enjoyment. Such behaviour was still encoded in his and Hea's distant memory, when they both needed physical envelopes to experience becoming.

"It seems like only yesterday. Your fur was so silky, so smooth. I really enjoyed touching you. The physical you, I mean…"

They rose a few thousand gorokos leaving Hia to experience the new environs on her own. Ham found it a little unnerving that the memories of his own past were quite so vivid. Hea was his love for long millennia, dating back to the last time they occupied physical bodies. She was beautiful then, and she's beautiful now, he thought, being well aware that she could read everyone of his thoughts. They were long past the stage of trying to shield their consciousness from each other. Since Hia was born, their unity seemed solidified into a single entity, which only they could tell apart. To other Hu embodiments, they were as one. Inseparable, consummate entity. After all, isn't that what true love is all about? Becoming one?

He scanned the planetary thought-waves to see if there was anything particular that Hia should learn. As he spread himself over the ages, his consciousness picked up the essence of Earth's past. He was utterly amazed.

"Did you know, darling, that Canines were only the second race to reach subconscious awareness?"

"Don't tell me it was the Broo… Men," Hea replied, giggling at her own joke.

"Well, in a way it had been Man," Ham replied, his tone serious yet, in a way, disbelieving his own conclusions. "Throughout history there have been embodiments of Hu, yes, here on Earth, who told Man the truth."

"And?"

"And throughout history, Man has rejected it." There was sadness in his voice. "Can you imagine? They rejected the Truth!"

For a while there was silence between them. Silence such as only outer space can offer. Devoid of noise, of sound, of thought. A void. A great emptiness.

Ham needed time to clear cobwebs from his mind. Then he looked at the contour of Hea, his wife, his love, his soul. The integral part of him that was, and will forever remain, inseparable part of him.

"There had been embodiments, teachers, prophets, who tried to pass on the truth they'd learned from Hu.

They tried different techniques. They gave Man the word, the example, the philosophy, the means to reach the Truth. Man rejected them all."

"But why...?" Hea was as filled with disbelief as Ham's thoughts felt. "How could they? Is that why the Canines now lead them on a leash?"

"Well, it's a long story. About three million years. Even as Hu developed a new physical enclosure, later the most magnificent brain in the system, Man opted out for matter over Hu. The children were born with fantastic ability to learn, to absorb knowledge. But, over the years, first their parents, then their educational systems, destroyed that capacity. By the time they reached 20 solar rotations, their ability to absorb new facts was brought down to a trickle. It was as if there was no room in their minds for anything new. The new and the old were on collision course."

Even as Hea listened, part of her mind made a time trip through the archives of the human race. As she scanned the past, her emotions began to feel the pain, which she sensed in Ham. The pain grew even as he shared his thoughts with her.

"They killed them, didn't they?"

Ham nodded. "The killed them. Pretty much all of them. The truth they taught had nothing to do with technology, money, material reality. Just the opposite. They don't seem to know, even now, that physical reality is illusory. That atoms are virtually empty space. That the true reality exists only in our minds and hearts..."

"They killed them for that?"

Once again, the universe they occupied was filled with silence. There was nothing Ham could add to Hea's last question. She knew the answer. Slowly, very slowly, they began the descent towards their daughter. She's left the Canines and the Man and swooped over fields filled with cornflowers. Even as she moved, a breeze seemed to follow her, swaying the cornfield to and fro, like a vast sea of blue.

"Mommy, Dad, you're back!" Hia's thoughts were filled with joy. "Have you ever seen such beauty as here?"

Millennia have past since Mars was filled with such gifts of Hu. Their kind was now given to enjoy the whole solar system. Regardless of climatic conditions. Since they shed their physical envelopes, they could travel anywhere and everywhere.

"When she matures, I must take her to the rings of Saturn," Ham mused, his thoughts filled with love for his daughter.

"You and I, together," Hea agreed, merging into his presence. And then she thought of the Brooho they left behind; the Man being led on a long leash by two beautiful Canines.

"Poor Canines," she thought, losing a fraction of her daughter's joy. "They still have a while to go. But at least they are on the right track."

"Poor Man," Ham thought, but this time he blocked his musings from his wife and daughter. "They had their chance and blew it."

"Oh, Mommy, Mommy, look!"

At the edge of the field they saw a tired looking Man following some distance behind three beautiful Canines. Their fur was golden, like the stems that supported the corn. Suddenly, the three Canines took off at a gallop, diving into the cornfield. The Man went frantic. He began swinging his arms, shouting, whistling, practically becoming apoplectic. From their vantage point, Ham, Hea and Hia could see that the Canines were chasing after some furry critter, which reached a burrow, and dove headlong into it.

The Canines sniffed for a moment or two, stretched their lithe bodies, and made their way back to the Brooho, to the Man, who by now was wiping perspiration from his forehead. Seemingly exhausted, he slid onto his heals.

Wagging their tails, the biggest of the Canines licked the Man's hand, then his face. The Man embraced the golden beast and seemed overjoyed.

"He must have thought he'd get lost in the field without them," Hie said. She looked really sorry for the Brooho.

"I wonder what he's doing there, with them. He doesn't seem to pick up any brooh at all." Hea seemed pensive.

"I think they are still training him. His not even on a leash yet. Must be still wild. I suppose, out here, in open fields, he can't really run away, can he?"

Then they relaxed. The Canines sat down, waiting for the Man to recover.

"They are really nice to him, aren't they?"

Ham and Hie nodded. Indeed they were.

***

Sphinx
or a Tale of
Cats, Mysteries, and Ducks

Felis Silverstris Catus
—about then I became.
Way back, in ancient Egypt
—it was my true domain.
My image was cast in stone.
Massive. Colossal. To last.
For future generations.
Presumptuous?
.....My influence was vast!

Then I became heavenly.
As Mafdet well... divine.
Later with grace abundant,
I became goddess Bast.
They changed my name so often...
frankly, it was a shame,
Yet—not being a rose
—what is there in a name?

I also ruled souls in India
—you'll find me in Mahabharata.
I dodged sword of Ezekiel;

had Welsh king Dda pass law…
just to protect my skin.
Ah, those were the days of fun…
(I'm not boring you, am I?
My story's almost done).

At long last I grew tired.
I also grew fur—rich 'n black.
Once baffling Nefertiti
(and other kings and queens),
now I'm in charge of mysteries.
I rule witches and quacks.
And should you not believe me,
I'll turn you into ducks.

***

(Inspired by Bozena Happach's steotite sculpture: Sphinx)

Two of a Kind

Whatever I did was wrong. It was too high, or too low; too much too the left, or to the right, or to anywhere. I couldn't even sit in my favorite place. Or I didn't smell right. Or I ate too much. Or I ate too loud! And all this in the first twenty-four hours. I mean, really. This is my home. I live here. This is my castle. I only invited her in out of, well... I'd been a bit lonely. What, with Brad and Mary out all day, I had no one to talk to. Or to play with. It's not easy...

Anyway, there was no pleasing her. Squawk, squawk, squawk.

"Aren't you ever happy about anything?" I asked.

"Hisssss..." she replied.

"And the same to you," I barked.

It got so bad that, after due consideration, I wished I'd never met her. I wished I hadn't brought her in, invited her indoors, showed her to Mary. I knew Mary would know what to do with her. She did. She cleaned her up, patched her bleeding paw and left ear, gave her milk, mashed some of the biscuits she'd bought for me and, well, and let her sleep it off. Whatever 'it' was, but it must have been some fight. I suppose her bleeding must have been what made me invite her inside in the first place. Some big brute must have taken advantage of her.

Must have been another cat. Probably a female.

Amazingly, the next day she was as bad as new. You've heard me. Black and white patches connected by an obnoxious character from which hung razor sharp nails. I won't mention her teeth. A royal pain. That's when the complaints had started in earnest. Higher, lower, left, right, pass the biscuits. Haven't you had enough? I might have put up with that. But… the furniture was scratched, she peed on the carpet, and tore part of the curtain. No kidding, in one day. When Brad came back from work, he threw her out. Physically. It's a wonder she didn't scratch his eyes out. The racket she'd made! You'd think she'd never been outdoors.

As far as I was concerned, she was guilty but insane. Mollifying circumstances?

I saw her again a week later. Sort of pressed into a tree, as though she wanted to be inside it. I don't believe she managed to stay dry. It had been pouring throughout the night. She must have been soaked through and through. Now, there was a proud one—she didn't even glance at the window. Not once. She seemed reconciled to her fate. Wet and hungry. And I bet, lonely. What a shame she had such a lousy character.

Still, what would you do? Let her die? I started scratching at the windowpane.

"I'll let you out the moment it stops raining, Johnny. Promise," I heard Brad's voice over my shoulder. They never understood what I was trying to tell them. Humans, the Homo sapiens, are not as sapient as you might think. They talk a lot but they seldom say anything of value. Except for Mary. She is something…. As for understanding my body language? Nada. Not a chance. Especially Brad. If I wanted to go out I would have brought the leash and held it out to him. Here and now, I was pointing. POINTING! I would have thought it was obvious.

"There, there," I pounded the glass, "under the tree..."

"I told you," Brand's voice was louder. "The moment it stops raining!"

It was no good. I curled up for a nap. What was a guy to do? I cannot walk through the glass, although I'd tried once. The stupid glass was so clean I couldn't see it. It reflected the bushes outside and I could swear I was just about to dive between them. Then—bang! It hurt, like a real wall. Later I'd learned that I've been lucky. My cousin managed to walk through a terrace window in pursuit of a black cat and bled for a week. Not from the cat; from the broken window. That was when I got interested in cats, only I decided, there and then, never to chase one. Whenever I was ready to pounce, my cousin's bleeding neck and hindquarters somehow stood before my eyes. It was like a warning from up above.

Anyway, we did go out that day and by the time we got back, What's-her-name was gone. That's what I called her. After all, she'd never introduced herself. No manners. Just squawked and hissed a lot. That's when she wasn't eating my food. I hated the little What's-her-name, but what, with the weather and all...

Somehow I knew this wasn't the end of it. There is such a thing as destiny, you know. Some people are meant for each other. And not just people....

What's-her-name was back a week later. It was a beautiful day and the doors to the terrace were left open.

Actually, it's more than a terrace. There is some lawn, a couple of trees, and a bit of a rock garden. When Brad and Mary first brought me home, I imagine they thought they could just let me out and save themselves a walk. Well, ha, ha. I remember the first thing my father told me.

"Son," he'd said, he had a marvelous deep voice, "remember son, never shit on your own doorstep."

Actually he'd said "never poop", I was little then. And he meant your own doorstep or garden or the place you live in, of course. As for walks, well, we have to go for walks. We must mark the trail, mark the trees, lampposts, curbs, bushes. We have to mark our territory and, sometimes, mark our way back. Marking the region is a rite, not a voiding of body fluids. If I wanted to just urinate I would use the powder room, like they do. When I think of all their scent going down the toilet.... What a waste!

Anyway, they often leave the doors open on Saturdays. The terrace is well fenced in, for my sake I suppose, but the fence was no barrier for What's-her-name. She squeezed through, between some loose boarding and just lay there, sunning herself. After a while I brought her a chunk of meat I dug out from the garbage bin. Nothing much, but What's-her-name was small, not like a dog, though today she looked sort of swollen. She sniffed the meat, and then seemed to swallow it in a single gulp. The girl was starving. I mean, really.

I had to play it just right. If I told Brad about her, she would go flying over the fence. I waited for Mary and me to be alone. Then I gently tugged at her till she came out onto the terrace. She'd spotted What's-her-name at once.

"Aren't you the naughty girl who peed on my carpet?" she asked. A reasonable question, I thought.

What's-her-name didn't move. Then she looked away. Innocent?

"I suppose you're hungry again?"

A rhetorical question. I think the feline could eat a horse and think nothing of it. She was like a garbage disposal unit.

What's-her-name kept looking away. She would never admit that she couldn't cope on her own. Why are cats so proud? I would have wagged my tail pronto just to show my appreciation. What-her-name? She was above it all. And... she'd just swallowed a chunk of meat I gave her.

Mary came back with a saucer of milk. What's-her-name studied it for a little while, sort of carelessly, then licked it clean. I mean, really clean. She did the same with the second saucer. Then, you'll never believe it, she cleaned up a good part of *my* supper!

OK. Enough is enough. I had to say something. I wooffed.

"Easy, boy," Mary said softly. "She's pregnant. She's eating for three or four. Maybe five or six. Maybe...."

Good grief! She's going to have kittens!

She came back a week later. Mary put a box outside, on the terrace, covered it with plastic, in case of rain, cut a hole out for a door, and put a rug on the floor for comfort. I wouldn't mind sleeping in it myself, if I could squeeze myself in. Only I was ten times What's-her-name's size. Anyway, I don't sleep with girls, not since Brad took me to a vet two years ago. And talking of Brad, he didn't like the arrangement. Not even on the terrace. Men are a lot tougher than women. Sort of harder inside. Mary? Mary was all sweet and cuddly. And pretty. And nice. Brad was a man's man. Macho. Only a week later he wasn't such a machismo any more....

There were six of them. Blind as bats. They crawled all over their mother, all over Mary, and, within hours, all over me. You'd never believe it. I was just lying there, making sure What's-her-name was safe in her box, when the first one came out and a made a beeline straight for my stomach. The next thing I knew, it, the soft furry ball, was nestled in my fur, somewhere between my hindquarters and my stomach. I couldn't move for hours. Well, minutes, but it seemed like hours. I could only just feel it, but I was afraid to move. I might squash the blighter or something.

Later that day Mary said that the weather forecast was for a cool night, with the possibility of ground frost and flurries. You've guessed it. The box and caboodle was moved to the downstairs powder room. Brad run out to buy a cat litter box. He came back with cans of food, biscuits and a dozen toys for the little ones.

"They are not coming out of the powder room till they learn to use the box," he said sternly. He looked about as stern as I'd ever seen him. Which is not much.

Later that evening three of them fell asleep on his lap, and he wasn't even in the powder room at the time. Men! Brad also had rented and old movie he wanted to watch on TV that night. I'm not much for movies. I preferred watching the kittens crawling everywhere they shouldn't.

He pressed the button. Soft, wistful music filled the room.

"Not too loud. You'll wake them," Mary said pointing at two of the kittens. The movie was a classic, starring Al Pacino and Michelle Pfeiffer. Frankie and Johnny.

Johnny: *So, how about you? Do you ever want to kill yourself sometimes?*
Frankie: *Yeah, everybody wants to kill themselves sometime.*

"Can you imagine being pregnant, wet, cold, starving and nowhere to go?" Brad's voice seemed filled with wonder as if he couldn't believe his own words. I could swear I heard a frog in his throat.

"No dear, I really can't," her eyes drifted to the black and white mother purring softly at her feet, her children having disposed themselves over various part of my anatomy. "Not with you around," she added so softly that I could only just make out her words.

"She's going to stay," she said a little louder. "Isn't she?"

"I think we should call her Frankie," Brad said pensively. "She and Johnny seem two of a kind," he added as an afterthought.

I had no idea why. I couldn't stand What's-her-name. Two of a kind??? Frankie? I'm the nicest of chaps. Frankie and Johnny? Visions of torn slippers, shredded newspapers and some broken saucers flashed before my eyes. I may have had my moments when I was a young mutt, but now? And anyway I'm not a mutt. I am black all-over. A jet-black Lab.

I collapsed on the carpet in utter desperation.

Moments later, Frankie got up, stretched herself leisurely, and walked towards me with careful, measured steps. She looked as if she owned the place. Then, very slowly, she cuddled up against me. I couldn't even see her, but I felt the warmth of her body. She was soft and she smelled just right. I bet they couldn't tell where she ended and I began. Except for the white patches. I didn't dare to move. Maybe she did own…

Naaah . . . no way.

On the other hand, never, never did she pee on the carpet again.

***

Sharing

Strrrrretching ... is rather nice. I felt sure that if I tried just a little harder, I could reach that flowerpot. I wouldn't, needless to say, knock it over. One simply doesn't do things like that. Anyway, it would be rather noisy, and frankly, noise—I do not like. If he hadn't trimmed my claws again, I am sure I could do it. Reach the pot, I mean. It is a nuisance. Sure my claws got caught now and then in something or other. But now, after the pedicure, or manicure to be more precise, I feel shorter by at least a couple of feet. Spoil sport! It's not as if I was ever running up and down the curtains. Well—almost... 'ever', and he does need new ones anyway. "So?"

Oh, well. Might as well take a little nap, I suppose. I haven't quite finished that dream I started this morning. I wonder just how it will end. Nnyahhh... actually yawning is rather nice, also. Aahhh, that is much better.

Oh-ho! I have a feeling that Stephan forgot something again. What a birdbrain! He'll get up too late and then rush out, as though the house was on fire. He never did like mornings very much. Rush, rush.... He will be in a hurry, of course, when he returns. But if I get in his way, at the door, I might get a couple of strokes down my spine and a scratch just below the ear. It took me ages to teach him the exact spot. But I must say, he was trying hard.

He is getting close now. Oh my! He is in a bit of a huff! Maybe I'd better unload him a bit. All right - onto the door! Once more onto the br....

He simply loves to brag that everybody thinks that only dogs can do that, but HIS Bartholomew does it without fail. Big deal. After all, dogs greet their Masters at the door *only* because it is expected of them, so why not? If he had only said that he gets such a big kick out of it, I would have done it right from the start. Sure, it is a pity to occasionally interrupt a nice dream just for a short trip to the door. But, there again, the sort of warm glow he positively oozes when I do it for him beats any dream I ever had.

Anyway, there is nothing a dog can do that I can't. Normally, a lot better! I can even wag my tail. What a stupid habit! I suppose, I can't really blame them, though. Some canine twit must have started it God knows how many eons ago, and now, if they don't wag their stupid tails, nobody believes that they are happy.

It's like people smiling. Why stretching one's lips from ear to ear should indicate a happy state, I shall never know. Often it looks positively painful, almost scary.

Especially, when some of them seem to have teeth twice the size of their mouths.

Now a gentle purrrr—makes sense. It sets up vibrations from my throat, through my spine, right to the tip of my tail. Well, almost. Oops—here he comes!

"Not now, Barth, I am in a hell of a hurry. Forgot the stupid . . . oh, all right, just a quick one then . . . that is nice . . . isn't it? O.K., and behind the ear—all right, all right, I know—a bit lower down. Now let me go. Must rush. Happy dreams. Bye!"

So much for my personal elocutionary giant. Anyway, it works every time. I get a quick scratch where I can't very well reach myself, whilst he stops feeling sorry for himself for being such a birdbrain. (No offence birds - just a figure of speech.)

And this figure of speech business.

One cannot but feel sorry for them. Not the birds. People. For such a long time they concentrated on being so verbose, that real communication seems to be completely beyond their capability. They have lost it. And the poor babies. I've seen only one, mind you. But the poor blighter couldn't say a word yet, and the darling mother would yap her head off at him. The baby, that is. So, obviously, he was doing his damnedest to communicate with her, but she wasn't even listening. Yap, yap, yap. Coochee coochee, cooo.... Really! Poor people. If only they stopped talking, they might hear something. Not words, of course, but real contact.

However, it might not be too late yet. After all, when I first met Stephan, I couldn't get through to him at all. Not for at least a whole year. But I do rather like him so I never gave up. I kept trying. First, I had to show him that I could hear him when he was not talking. It wasn't easy. I kept repeating the same actions, round and round, until the bright lad (sorry, I don't mean to be sarcastic, but it was rather tedious) began to notice that I seemed to know some of his intentions in advance. I could hardly fail, since he was broadcasting them for half an hour, before the thoughts even formulated in his own mind.

Then he became aware that I could tell when he was coming home. The fellow didn't realize that when he was nearing our apartment, he stood out like a blaring beacon in the middle of the Sahara desert. Not that I've ever seen a desert, but he has talked about it.

And that's another thing.

When Stephan described this desert to his friends, it was such an inadequate image of what was in his mind. If people would only stop talking and listen—instead. Still, Stephan does have such a vivid imagination. His friends would really enjoy his images. I do. But when he and his friends get together, it sounds more like a waiting game. Each waiting to jump in with his or her own story, the moment one of them stops to catch a breath.

Well, I am not giving up on my Stephan. I can't explain it, but I have a feeling that somehow, soon, something will happen, that will make a big difference in our relationship. Maybe I am psychic—my tail has been tingling like never before. In fact, it makes me a bit nervous. I hope he doesn't notice. He would never understand. Anyway, not yet.

"The need for sharing is a strange desire. Success resulting from adamant pursuit of ideas generated by an inquisitive mind loses its joy, when contained in an emotional vacuum. The vision and the will to scale ever more challenging crags, to see beyond the furthest horizons, become shrouded with a myopic veil. The need to share is inherent to the success of crossing the boundaries of human perception. The crossing of the turbulent waters of intellectual limitation, and feeling the freedom this act affords, is the real measure of success."

The notes he'd received from his astrologer friend vaguely amused him. Not that he put much faith in her arcane prognostications. The script was heavy on the esoteric, slightly pompous, and light on facts he could use in everyday life.

Stephan glanced at Bartholomew curled up at his feet. His furry friend seemed oblivious to the world around him. Stephan grinned when he became aware of the vibration, a gentle purr, where the cat was touching his left calf. Somehow old Barth managed to share his pleasure in a most inconspicuous way.

Stephan returned to his reading.

"You are, my dear Stephan, blessed with the Midas touch, though the substance you crave is more precious than mere glitter and sheen of gaudy if rare metal. You dare to defy the expected, to lead where others often failed to follow. But you will not be denied. You have already crossed the solitary isthmus joining the known and the forbidden...."

It was getting late. A hard day in the office often left him on the very edge of dozing off. Even as he closed his eyes, the loose sheets of paper floated down to his feet like autumn leaves. His mind took off on a tangent of its own. Midas, he mused, a blessing . . . a curse?

His thoughts, over which he lost all control, drifted still further into the kingdom of Phrygia in the Anatolian

Highlands. He was swept by a strange feeling of enchantment.

Surely, he thought, this is too real to be just a dream....

As the curse would have it, he held his ground. He climbed the steps of success, each breeding the next, each balanced precariously, yet offering foothold enough to jump to the next rung of insatiable desire to climb still further....

Stephan felt lost. Where am I, he mused with the remaining fragments of his awareness. Anatolian Highlands?

He looked over his shoulder and . . . an anxious tremor touched his heart. He did not understand it at first. Yet it grew stronger with each fresh step he took on his precarious journey. Then the haze of apprehension cleared and he knew. He was alone. He had fought too hard to retrace his steps. He had been too close to stop, even to rest. Yet he needed to share. And there was no one.

The need for sharing is a strange desire... the awareness he'd left behind repeated. Didn't I just read something like that....

Thus onward he went, and as he reached and looked over the most turbulent crest he glimpsed, he felt, he sensed—Eden. He saw Paradise. He grasped and he held fast with the churning hunger of unquenched desire.

That last step had been his doom.

Now he could never turn back. His voice could no longer reach down to the valley which he had left behind. He could now show the way, a path much easier for others to follow... but no one would hear. He needed to share the greatest of all successes, to share the greatest prize....

His heart, ebullient with the glory of his achievement, could no longer contain its joy. Consequently, even as a sun heated beyond its limits explodes with the fury of Nova, so Stephan's emotions, imbued with the joy of the final success, restrained only by the brittle mantle of his solitude, could contain its forces no longer.

With shattering might his inner heart exploded. For a split second the universe around him was suffused with the rays of joy. In areas remote, remote and aloof, people felt a sudden warmth of contentment, not knowing why, but smiling in return. Nearer, strangers embraced each other and laughed, yet soon turned away embarrassed, for they too were ignorant of the cause for their amity.

Such is the power of joy, a voice said. Who's voice, he wondered unaware of its source.

When Stephan came to, he was covered in sweat. Whatever had happened in his dream was much too real for comfort. Somehow, in his altered awareness he'd taken this final step of understanding. Nevertheless, it was neither his mind nor body that shared this experience. His heart ruled supreme in that realm. In that realm, the power to feel reached far beyond the limits of analytical comprehension. Yet it was utterly overwhelming. It drained him of all his energies. The great vacuum tore at him from all directions at once. To fill with what, he wondered? Love? Emotions? Surely, not just the ability to share? Still in that intangible reality, to safeguard his sanity, he withdrew his vigilance into a protective cocoon, and in so doing, he released the unrequited emotions that swelled within him. Then, spent and exhausted, he suffered merciful Morpheus to claim his wholly drained awareness.

Still feeling drowsy, he adjusted his armchair to a reclining position, made sure that Bartholomew was still at his feet, and, once again drifted into a slumber. He needed rest, not somnambular nightmares.

This was not his day....

Soon yet another strange dream took hold of his troubled mind. A dream real—yet timeless, intense—yet strangely gentle. He had dreamed of dreaming . . . and within that dream he rose above his body and looked down at the reclining semblance. How frail and hapless is a human frame. When spirit deserts it—but an empty shell, a mass of swirling atoms destined for perdition.

As Stephan hovered in the intense reality of his gossamer existence, he felt invaded by an alien touch. A touch of amusement? He wanted to hide in the sanctuary of his sleeping body, but curiosity prevailed. He opened his guard . . . and the gentle smile was there again to greet him.

"Welcome, my friend and Master," he felt the emotive thoughts, "I waited for you . . . I knew you could listen."

And Stephan was afraid again, but the gentleness of the prodding thoughts bore neither malice nor danger. He opened more, a little... and then he saw Bartholomew. The regal sphinx was sitting erect, poised as though cut from velvety marble. His shimmering eyes did not look at the reclining body, but were fixed to the spot where Stephan's awareness had risen. The feline eyes were glowing with open joy and comfort. Was Bartholomew smiling? Was there amusement in his eyes? Do cats really smile?

"Oh yes, they do," his patient friend purred softly. "I have been smiling at you all along. A smile is a state of mind, not a baring of teeth!"

"You are Bartholomew, and I hear you!" Stephan thought aghast as though needing to compound conviction.

"Of course you do, why are you so surprised? Can you not hear the plants growing? Does not a rose smile at you with her blooming petals?"

And Stephan, silent, listened. He listened to his heart and to all the hearts that beat with the inherent yet still unconscious desire to give of oneself to each other, to join in their becoming, to join their singularity into a cosmic embrace of unified existence....

....and he felt wisdom that transcends all that intellect can muster . . . the illusion of successes melted into a bliss of pure knowledge, into the naked joy of timeless state of being. And then Stephan realized that for the first time in his life he was truly awake. And he felt joy—again...

....and he was sharing.

***

Dreamax

"**Never! Not in a million years!**" Fred rolls up his soulful eyes, as only he knows how. "Believe me, mother. Not in a million years!"

Yap, yap, yap... I believe him. After all, Dreamax Inc. had only begun its operations two years ago. It should not have effected us. Any of us. At least, not yet. Not if we were reasonably careful.

The explanation for the Dreamax's instant, unprecedented success is fairly obvious: the vast majority of the master race had grown, understandably, bored. I mean sssoooo bored—with their daily, dull routines. Eight to four, nine to five, ten to six. Whatever. The gray, mulling masses would do anything, to escape their self-imposed doldrums. Frankly, I don't blame them. Had they only learned to relax....

Sorry, I digress. The question is what are we going to do about Max? As long as tapping on Alpha rhythms had been limited to, pardon me, wild zoo animals, it didn't matter. Much. But since they tried the hook up on Max.... The son of a bitch always talked too much. The bigger they are, the more noise they make. Doesn't say much for his breading, really. Must have been on his father's side. Anyway, if the master race learned the truth about us, the good old days would be over. Probably for good. We must, MUST, find a way out of this jam.

"You shouldn't call him a son of a bitch." Fred always stands up for his younger brother. Not that Max needs much protection. "Not you, mother!"

I let that pass. "Did you actually speak to Max about it?" I ask. Fred is the one who went past the clinic by car, with Barbara, and overheard Max right there, at the clinic.

"That's the first thing I did. I'm not stupid, you know. But Max, well, he talks...." Fred moves his handsome head from side to side, seemingly at a complete loss.

That's quite true. Max is too young to know that he can modify his Alpha rhythms. Like everything else, the Alpha rhythms vary, in cycles per second. Eight to thirteen, I am told. For crying out loud, nobody intelligent would count them. You just know. You sense it. With practice. You can raise the cycles so that it's near impossible for anyone to hear you. No matter what the equipment.

It is time for a momentary lapse in communication. Nothing profound had ever been accomplished on an empty stomach. Barbara just returned and that means instant chow. Max will keep. He can't fly away. My goodness, he can't even run away!

Poor Max....

That's it!

"We have to organize his escape." I say, without moving a muscle. I like doing that. If we hadn't learned subliminal thought transfer, they would have been onto us long ago.

Fred looks pleased, very pleased, with my suggestion. It's so simple. Why hadn't I thought of it before? Why should I have. There is no law that says that I, and I alone, have to come up with *all* the bright ideas. I'm a professional mother, not some pompous solon with an over-inflated ego.

That evening, long after the kids and even Barbara and her hubby retired, the three of us, Fred, Bulky and myself, set out for the Dreamax building. There is nothing much I can actually do myself, but someone has to keep an eye on the two youngsters. Fred can be trusted, but Bulky... well, Bulky is a bit—bulky. In more ways than one. He tends to overpower anyone in his direct path. Mostly, with affection. Both lads are quite sharp, for their age, but their principle strength lies in the fabulous agility of their slim, muscular bodies. Not of their brain cells. If I can only keep them quiet, all will be safe and sound. Quiet.

Must keep them quiet.

A little past midnight, a single, loose cedar board swings silently sideways. A pair of shining, cautious eyes peers left then right, then detaches itself from the dark fence in a mad dash for the nearest tree. Two more dark, nervous shapes follow, mere shadows, against an even darker background. We walk in single file, studying the territory ahead, then darting against an assortment of fences and hedges spanning between patches of irregular, deeper obscurity of mature, sidewalk elms. The street lamps, normally offering a welcome sense of relief and security, on this occasion punctuate areas of dire danger.

"This is a commando mission. It's serious. Dead serious. If anyone of us gets caught, we might well end up in circumstances a lot worse than the one we are attempting to resolve," I told them before we started. I meant every word.

After six blocks, we begin closing in on downtown. We increase our pace. Success breeds confidence. Excessive confidence, folly. The next moment we scramble, head over heels, towards the darkest shadows we can find. We spend the next fifteen minutes shaking, otherwise paralyzed. Four pairs of fiery monsters came upon us, suddenly, in quick succession. All four cars were speeding like crazy, full headlights cutting sharp, painful scars in the serene darkness. I hate glaring headlights. I hate glaring. For ten minutes, I can't see a thing. Totally blinded. You simply don't expect four drunks to be gallivanting at high speed, in a small, sleepy town, after midnight. I'm scared breathless. I start panting like a bitch in heat. At least, the near miss got the boys quiet. That helped. You can't possibly guess who might be listening. At any time some stupid cat might start screaming, some flea-bitten insomniac—barking. We have to be very quiet. To top it all, Bulky almost twisted his ankle. Well, he is bulky, after his father. After that, I change the rules. I lead the way, the boys stay behind till I call them, silently, to follow.

The rest of the way we advance a lot more slowly, more cautiously. It's safer.

The Dreamax Inc. Headquarters, like all its branches,

had been designed for easy access. A three storey, dark red brick building, the main floor about five feet above the sidewalk. The raised entry level is where the clients make their selections. Lions, panthers, an assortment of wild cats, a few exotic bears, a number of apes and monkeys. I heard that the clientele preferred the carnivores. More thrilling, bloody. People like that. After the patients make their selection, they climb to the second or third floor, lie down, and get hooked up to the never-never land. For the next three, four hours, they tap the genetic memory of the lions or bears, or whatever, vicariously sating their own, atavistic need for excitement, long missing from their pathetic, exploitative, dull lives.

The half basement houses mainly offices and labs. According to my information, Max had to be kept on the main floor. The building offers, from our point of view, a dubious advantage of staying open 24 hours-a-day. Easy enough to get in, a lot harder not to be spotted. Then, I have an idea. All we have to do, is to wait for some customers to arrive and then, we'll saunter in, quite openly, pretending to be with them. That's it.

The three of us crouch under the flight of stairs leading to the main entrance. For the moment, I feel quite relaxed, safe. A single light over the door adds to a sense of security by cloaking us in an even deeper shadow. All we can do, now, is wait. Then Bulky gives me a scare. He starts scratching himself as though he's being eaten alive. He may well be, but we are on a mission. I'm afraid he'll fall over himself and make some sort of a racket. Kids have no control, these days.

As luck would have it, in hardly any time, a sad looking, dejected, thirty-something girl, strolls past us to the front door. I nudge Fred. He can keep quiet enough when he knows it to be important. He falls in step with the melancholy stranger, and slips in quite naturally. The girl must think he lives in the building. The sleepy receptionist assumes, quite naturally, that Fred came in with the girl. He did, the receptionist is half right. Not a bad score.

For a moment I'm afraid Fred will start indulging in some overly friendly behavior towards the visiting woman. Fred does suffer from a slightly perverted sense of humor. Or maybe, it is just his sense of compassion, but he cannot resist demonstrating his congenial nature even, if not in particular, towards total strangers. Or is it mostly towards women? I told him not to be so promiscuous, but there is only so much a mother can do.

Fred is in. The night restores the briefly disturbed silence. Nights, in our town, usually are quiet. Very quiet. Barring accidents, we're on our way. The next visitor, looking as lost and bewildered as his predecessor, saunters in about ten minutes later. Bulky is at the prospective client's side in a single, silent leap, then, with a simulated indifference, trots inside the building. Once inside, he makes a beeline for the somber, underlit corridor. He follows Fred's direction. I wait.

Fred comes through first.

"At this rate we'll spend hours in here."

"So what's the hurry?" Bulky, slower but much more relaxed, wants to know.

"How about a nap?"

"Don't even think about it!" This comes as an urgent hiss.

It's time for me to cut in. "Both of you keep quiet. You are supposed to listen in for Max's thoughts, not fill the air with your own yapping. Have you located him yet?"

"Sorry, mother." Fred and Bulky whisper in unison. I smile. There's no such thing as a telepathic whisper. Not till now!

Max can't be far away but they keep over fifty different animals on the main floor. That takes a lot of space, but mostly it makes for an awful lot of subliminal clutter. From where I am hiding, all I can hear is an articulated hum.

At this stage, I still have no idea what is happening to or with Max. Since they kidnapped him, I had been worried stiff. Until Fred heard him. They had Max officially listed at the Dreamax clinic. At least he was safe. The next day I heard, on the TV, that some human derelict claimed to have been hooked up to Max. Luckily, the derelict in question, had a reputation of the town guzzler. Nobody listened much to him but he did make the local news. Local, but it did spell danger.

The old man, the drunk, expounded magnificently bizarre stories. He raved about us training men to behave in ways beneficial exclusively to our own comfort and existence. Now that is total, unadulterated twaddle. We think of man's welfare as much as we do of our own. We consider our relationship to be interdependent. Symbiotic. Surely, on occasion, we have to draw a line, but....

How long do I have to spend sitting here before the boys find Max?

Anyway, the priority is to remove Max from the Dreamax premises before anyone else gets a chance to confirm the old man's ranting. If the bizarre stories were to be confirmed, all hell would break loose. Man might learn the truth about us, and then? Dissection tables, here we come. Not funny.

I'm worried. Normally, I don't mind waiting. But I

am worried. The boys, alone... My thoughts are getting darker. I wish Max was back. I'm scared. For the first time in my life, I am afraid of man.

My mind reaches out to distant, arcane, immutable memories. I see a world, a beautiful world, all species roaming free, eating when hungry, on occasion licking their wounds—the penalty nature extracts for stepping into another's space. Then, I shiver. I see a zealot, a religious maniac, an aboriginal throwback, a psychopathic murderer, proclaiming man's superiority over nature. He tell his barbaric followers to subject nature to their own, twisted, perverted will.

Henceforth, man lives under an impression, that he, and he alone, holds monopoly on free thought. Man usurps supremacy, generally not by the use of his mind, but by total disregard of anyone who might lay claim to their rightful share of blessings that the earth has to offer. In such profusion! Through his insatiable greed, man brings the earth to the very brink of destruction. Even as man overcomes his desire to implement the hundred fold overkill capability of eradicating all life with his atomic gadgetry, he continues to remain quite oblivious to the demands which nature places upon him. If man cannot poison the earth with radiation, he tries, with equal determination, to poison, the giver of all life, with the absurd profusion of his waste. Earth is drowning in man's excrement.

I am growing afraid of man.

Man uses his mind to make gadgets. We and our kinfolk, continue to develop ourselves in different ways. We grow on the within. Not on the without, like man. We do not grow in quantity. We develop in quality. That's right. We are not human.

I wish something would happen. This is nerve racking.

All life forms had been free, once. Now, I can see rows upon rows of hapless rabbits, held in medieval fetters, their heads immobilized. I see men, dressed in white coats, spraying noxious poison into the shackled rabbits' eyes. Eyes held open by mechanical contraptions. Man is testing toxicity of mascara or some other make up, for the philandering whores of the human kind. Don't ever call them bitches. They are of a human perversion. Two rabbits break their backs, vainly attempting to escape their agony. They fail. Man is bigger, stronger. The master.

I am afraid for my boys.

I can see thousands of animals raised, bread exclusively for slaughter. They never had a chance to live before dying. They were born, lived and were quartered—in fetters. To satisfy man's obsession with eating. The masters of this earth?

For man to grow fatter.

I am afraid for my boys.

Millions of chicken, scared, terrified, balancing precariously on a wire floor. Their space confined, unable to spread their wings. They cannot turn around. They are fed at one end, eggs collected at the other. For man to eat. To accumulate cholesterol. To grow fatter.

I am afraid for my boys.

Countless numbers of my kindred, cousins, writhing in agony, their bodies covered with sores. Experimental animals, injected with every disease known to man, virulent, painful, cancer, AIDS, venereal diseases, all caused by man's abuse of his and our environment. I see my brothers, sisters, slowly dissected, man's bloody hands protected by rubber gloves, our own kind dying, slowly, so slowly, to save man. So that man can grow fatter.

I am afraid for my boys.

Slaughter, mass slaughter. The superior species. The master race. The master murderers, torturers, deviants, debauchers—our friends.

Man has taken away our freedom, converted our planet to a monstrous, ever growing, fetid garbage dump and now is set to steal our minds. Our memories. We do not make gadgets. Our minds, our hearts, our memories— are all we have left.

It would be less tragic if it weren't for the fact that although man has considerably more gray matter in his overdeveloped, gadgetry cranium, he hadn't learned to use more then a minute fraction of it. Come to think of it, little babies can communicate with us by subliminal projection. I could call it telepathy, but the word implies something very cerebral and advanced, rather then fundamental, intrinsic. Alas, by the time babies learn to talk, they lose their ability. No wonder. You cannot talk and think at the same time. If you don't believe me, listen to anybody. Any man. Particularly those who talk a lot. Like some teachers, preachers, and particularly politicians. The more they prattle, the less sense they make.

No. We send our thoughts in their original form. Before they are converted into some strange, symbolic forms which, after all, is what words are all about. Each word carries, to every person, a slightly different meaning. I you are reading this, you see what I mean. If you are reading this, I must have been caught, fettered, my memories stolen, recorded. I don't know. Perhaps I learned, since, to block out that particular memory. For all I know, you don't even know what I am talking about.

Well, do you?
There!

In true telepathy you do not send words across, but that image which precedes the formulation of a word. A word is merely a symbol, a mere shadow of the idea itself. Some human mothers can, on occasion, communicate telepathically with their babies. But never by yapping nineteen-to-a-dozen! Once you substitute a symbol for the essence, for the real meaning, you can say bye-bye to subliminal transfer. Try it!

God, I'm afraid for my boys....

Dreamax still do not understand the method. They learned the trick, partially, by accident. A technician fell asleep, the electrodes on his head connected to a contraption still producing an electroencephalogram, the other end fixed to a snoring chimpanzee. When the technician came to, he swore he'd been in the jungle, swinging carefree on a tree, participating in all sorts of exiting monkey business. They soon learned that only in the Alpha rhythm cycle such transfer is possible. Rather than add true excitement to their own lives, man made the necessary gadgets.

The rest is history.

If they do not place us in shackles, fatten us for slaughter, inject us with poison, or dissect us live, to save their abused bodies, they will steal our memories. Man, the superior master, our best friend. A liar.

I admit to our own share of guilt. We have grown too complaisant. We have tolerated man's antics, partially, through our acquired laziness. We have grown accustomed to having all things done for us, our food brought, prepared, served, and the dishes cleaned. We've not only grown tame, but timid. Over the last few hundred generations we had done little more than to lie around, think, exchange ideas with our own kind, on occasion to stimulate man in his stagnant thinking. We feed some thoughts to men, normally during his or her sleep, we try to slow them down, to quiet the incessant noise for ever churning in man's under-controlled, scantily used brain. We tried, but, let's face it, not very hard. We had grown lazy. Too lazy.

"Don't push till I lift the hatch, you stupid mutt!" I catch Bulky's urgent thought. I jump, my head knocking the underside of the entry staircase.

They found Max. I never doubted they would. After all, they are my children. The smartest. If I don't tell them that, they will stay that way. I will not have them spoiled. My taut muscles are on fire. I must relax. I stretch out from the tip of my nose to the end of my tail.

"Shut up. Mother told us to keep quiet. Wait till we get out." That is Fred admonishing Max with his usual clear mind. My, how I love these boys. They are all I have left. Sure they get into hot soup, on occasion. Boys will be....

"Look out!" This is Max. "Someone is coming...."

I'm up on my feet. My spine feels prickly. Suddenly, I itch all over. If they hurt my boys, they're dead meat. Shouldn't talk like that. Can a mother help worrying? Oh, please, let them all get out safely. Please!

In the still of the night, the broken glass explodes like dry shrapnel in a small room. The noise comes from the direction of the side lane. It is magnified by the wall opposite.

"Run for it!" A scream.

I don't have to ask. I sense. The three lads are out through the window, head first, and down the lane like three black, galloping devils. My God! They jumped down from the first floor. I wish, incongruously, that I hadn't let them eat so much. Landing from fifteen feet on all fours can be quite tricky, if you're on the plump side. At least, the lads have spend the last months or two playing in the park with little Janny and Joey. I don't care what anyone says: human children are nice. Very nice. What a pity they always grow up. The exercise will come in handy, if the lab staff decide to give chase. Why am I thinking all these stupid thoughts?

I move rapidly to the other side of the street and wait. The Dreamax building looks as sleepy as I feel, or would feel, if it weren't for the adrenaline. It seems that no one is going to give chase. I wonder what scared the boys away in such a hurry.

I am the last to get home. I've done nothing and I feel dead tired. Nerves.

We meet in the garden. The boys are talking, all at the same time. From what I overheard before they noticed me, each had fought a mortal battle against overwhelming odds. They all won, of course. I can't help laughing. The sudden release of tension makes me very, very tired. I take a quick nap. When I wake up, surprise, they lads are still talking.

Thank God, it's over. The next day, I hear that there was a break-in at the Dreamax Inc. labs. God, how I hate labs. I hate labs. I hate irresponsible researchers. I hate doctors who charge for removing symptoms while ignoring the cause of the disease. I hate scientists who sublimate their conscience, I hate . . . I don't hate anybody. But I have to work on it. Some equipment and most of the exponents had been stolen from Dreamax. They are probably exaggerating. Bulky swears he opened only a dozen cages. Maybe the apes did the rest?

I take time to advise, through our extended subliminal communication network, that everyone should stay away from *any* Dreamax installations. Also, to prepare contingency plans, in case anyone, inadvertently, falls into enemy hands. That's right. Enemy. It is time to stand up for our rights. Enough is enough. They laid hands on my boy!

Finally, I tell them to start practicing switching off the Alpha rhythm. Consciously. In case they catch anyone in spite of our precautions. After we learn to control the rhythm at will, one of us will allow himself, or herself, to be caught - accidentally, of course. Once they find us useless transmitters, they'll leave us alone.

That's it.

Finally I am done. Finished.

I saunter over to my boys. As a stretch out, pretending to be taking a nap, I listen to their mushrooming stories. It is, as I'd expected. By now, the whole neighborhood knows, that Max, Fred and Bulky had battled innumerable opponents, attacked hordes, yes hordes, of the ungodly lab technicians, jumped from at least a six story window, breaking through headlong, in the process, a triple glazed, bullet proof, unbreakable glass. Then, they raced through the deserted streets, for miles, at something approaching the speed of sound, dodging dozens of pursuing cars with blaring sirens. The stories expanded exponentially. Day by day. While the memories are still fresh in my mind, I encode them in our racial genetic code. For posterity.

Life is back to normal. I lay back, occasionally taking a quick peek at the boys. In spite of their over-enthusiastic imagination, I can tell that all three keep a vigilant eye over little Janny and Joey. It is not the kids' fault that they're human. Perhaps, just perhaps, the course of evolution will raise man from his lonely, mental exile. Then, we shall all share our thoughts, our feelings, dreams, aspirations. There will be no need, then, of any Dreamax clinics. No one will be lonely, ever again. Perhaps....

Perhaps—is such a long time.

By then, my boys' exploits will be part of history. And a good yarn. Followed by a good nap. And a dream. My three boys....

***

A Bad Apple

You might as well know that every single story in this book has been recorded by either a cat or a dog. Sometimes both. We don't actually write them ourselves, but, when our well-meaning "masters" are asleep, we feed the stories directly into their subconscious, and then, on awakening, our human friends put them down on paper. Or on a computer screen. Memory. Computer memory. They don't always come out quite right, but, well, nothing is perfect in this world. It's not like in the Kingdom.

My name is Bartholomew, Bartek for short, and I've been a Cat for a long, long time. Or for many times, if you prefer. I've been responsible for bringing about many cute little bodies for dormice, and such like, to inhabit during their stay on Earth. Evidently, this must be, at least partially, the reason why now it is my job to take the little ones, the nascent states of consciousness, across the Great Divide.

It is not always easy.

People—they think otherwise—but they are the least advanced, the most reliant on material accoutrements. Oh, they may have a greater potential, but they don't use it the way they should. We, in the Animal Kingdom, we don't worry about tomorrow, about what we shall eat or drink, how we shall dress, or how to sustain our temporary physical envelopes.

Ahhh, there he is.

"Kaytek, come down."

The object of my attention, a young Cat who lost his life just yesterday, (of course there is no time here, not really), is hovering about ten feet above the ground between two branches of that oak tree in front of the house we'd both lived in—at different times, of course.

Now, I am not saying that all Cats and Dogs return to the Kingdom pronto, without stopping at go or going to jail. Some of us have problems. Mostly, we get too attached to the people we live with. Don't get me wrong. Some of them are nice. I mean, really nice. Maybe in their next life they'll be one of us.

Now, I have to explain all this to Kaytek. He is a small little Siamese, who got hit by a car. He shouldn't have been crossing that street; on the other hand the car shouldn't have been speeding. Anyway, we all pay our dues, so, right now, little Kaytek feels a little lost. So would you be if you'd been hit by a car bigger than a Hippopotamus, charging at you at 100 miles an hour. OK. Maybe just 50 miles, but that was enough to get little

Kaytek out of his physical envelope. Now, he's hovering, as I said, about ten feet above the ground, trying to hide behind the trunk of the oak tree I mentioned.

"Kaytek, you are safe now. Nobody's going to run into you…"

He doesn't quite trust me. After all, he'd never seen me in my body. I got this job before he was born. Now he looks me over, up and down, and climbs another two braches higher up. Can't blame him, not really; he's half my size. Not only. Kaytek is small, and in spite of his tremendous strength—skinny, very pale, though with beautiful dark brown points at his paws, ears, tail and, of course his face. Like all Siamese I, too, have even darker points but my fur is rich chocolate, so they don't stand out as much.

Anyway, I've got to explain to him that it is like the Good Book says. He put us all in Paradise, happy, blissfully happy, and then Adam, with just a little assistance from Eve, screwed it all up. Well, the Creator is a fair Spirit. He kicked them both out of Eden, but let the rest of us stay. Why not? We didn't eat any apple from any tree of knowledge. We remained innocent, unable to sin, to commit an error. I mean a willful error. Knowing that we are doing wrong. We all make errors. We're not perfect. But we don't make errors on purpose. Humans do. Often. Daily. It's called Ego. Whenever their Ego takes charge, they spin out of control. Poor guys. They shouldn't have eaten that apple. Now they're stuck. They cheat, steal, hate, murder… usually out of greed. Greed or fear. We don't do any of that. We don't know how to be greedy, decadent, selfish and all that. It takes knowledge to be evil. To say that you know better than the Spirit which created all the universes and everything and everyone in them. That takes an enormous Ego.

Kaytek is not moving an inch.

"Kaytek, nobody can hurt you. For a start, they can't see you. For…"

I'd better not tell him, not yet, that right now he's a spirit and a dozen elephants could run through him a leave him unharmed. Somehow cats don't seem to take kindly to be told that they don't have a body.

"You can see me!"

His voice is a little squeaky but at least he acknowledged my present. It's a start.

"Yes, but I'm like you."

That got him thinking.

"Like me?" Silence. "You got run over?"

Nah. That didn't work.

I could give him a whole song and dance about different vibrations creating different realities, but he's really too young. His last life was a dormouse. He was tiny, cleaver, sneaky and cute. He did everything right, they upgraded him to a cat. Who are "they"? Ask them. I'm new to this job. I just have to make sure he understands Bardo.

"Swing you paw at that branch in front of you."

"This one?"

The poor blighter swung his paw and it went right trough it.

"You're not sitting on it, Kaytek. It's all in your mind."

The air shimmered and Kaytek found himself smoothly, well, almost smoothly, descending to the ground. He landed about three feet in front of me.

"Do I know you?" he asked, seeming reconciled to the fact that the world around him went completely crazy.

"Yes, and, no," I answered in my best judicial tone of voice. As I was saying, I was doing my job. You know, like a bodhisattva, only in the transition reality.

Kaytek continued to stare at me, then, in a single leap he jumped at me, bounced of, and rolled a dozen somersaults along the lawn. I told you, I was at least twice his size. The grass, on the other hand, gave no frictional resistance to his present body.

"Ouch!" He sat on his hunches. "You are real," he declared, licking his hindquarters, which bumped into me. He couldn't control his body in flight.

"We are both in the same reality," I told him.

"Good!" he exclaimed. There was relief in his voice. Only in physical universe cats speak in subliminal whisper, humans call it telepathy, but it isn't. Anyway, here, in this transient reality, we have a choice to communicate directly or vocally. In the beginning, vocal is more reassuring.

Kaytek visibly relaxed, and began to examine the world around him with new interest. He noticed that, depending on his state of mind, imagination really, he could make grass either solid or void. It could either support his weight, or as with the branch on the oak, he could sink right into it. It would be funny to find oneself in Australia by mistake. For a while I just watched him.

"As a matter of fact," I said gently, more to reassure than instruct, "the same is true of the physical world. It's ninety-nine point nine-nine-nine-nine percent empty space. Void. We sustain it with our mind. Like here, only here we are less dependant on reality created by others."

"…ninety-nine point?"

"Decimal point. OK. Think of a large saucer full of water. Now put a drop of milk into it. Think of milk as solid matter. Now mix them together. The milk in the water is the amount of solid you get in matter."

"You're kidding," he said, his tone superior to my apparent ramblings. "That monster that hit me was no empty space."

As a matter of fact, it was, but I couldn't tell him that. He was not ready yet. You can't expect a mere kitten to deny a reality to which, or in which, he'd awoken a few thousand times, all at once. Kaytek continued to prod flowers, blades of grass. Then, before he realized it, his head got stuck in the trunk of the massive oak.

"Think empty?" I told him. There was a plop and his head came out.

"Holy Bastet! You're not kidding." And for the first time he looked at me with a smidgen respect. It doesn't come easy to a cat. "Who are you, ah, Sir?"

"Bartholomew. Bartek, if you like. I'll be putting you to sleep." By the way, for the uninitiated, since about 600 BC, a cat usually represented the goddess Bastet.

"But I'm not sleepy. I could go on like this..."

"Yes, I know. But it's not that kind of sleep. It is the sleep of Bardo. The place where we dream up new realities. You will dream of all sorts of wonderful things, many, many of them, and then..." Should I tell him that the worlds are infinite in number?

"But I'm not sleepy, Bartek. Ah, Bartholomew."

"...and then, one day, you'll wake up and try to remember that dream. And all the smells you imagined, and the tastes you thought of, and all the sounds you heard in your dream you'll really smell, and really taste and really hear in... well, in a new, fresh, beautiful body, into which nobody ever smashed a front bumper."

"B-b-but why?"

"Well, to experience life. Life, Kaytek, is the gift from the Spirit that lets us experience all our dreams. Life is change. Life shows us consequences of our actions. Life is real, not at all like a dream. Even a Bardo dream."

Kaytek keeps looking at me with those still youthful round eyes. He was hardly two when the car hit him. At that point I noticed that half his attention was drifting upwards. The next instant I was looking at him perched on the very top of the oak.

"Get a load of this view!" he shouted from above.

I shrugged. So much for his interest in Bardo. He didn't even ask what it meant. It wasn't going to be easy. When they leave their physical envelopes when still very young, they haven't had time to develop all sorts of fears, which restrict our freedom in the physical world. In fact, that's why we all leave our bodies, sooner or later, to start afresh. You might say that ultimately, fear is the death of everyone. By scanning his past, I saw that Kaytek was not afraid of anyone or anything. Paradoxically, that's what cost him his life.

And what a lovely cat his was. Still is, of course.

With a single thought I raised myself to his level and sat on thin air looking at him, while he was holding onto a branch for his life. I think this is when it all clicked. Slowly, very slowly, he let go of the oak. We both drifted downwards, a few feet at a time, till we landed on the lawn.

"You're serious, aren't you, Sir?" That respect was growing in his voice. Actually, he didn't speak. I felt his emotive thoughts.

I told him about the world. "In the beginning..." you know the story. God created... The thing that we all forget is that Eden covered the whole Earth. From sea to shining sea. From ocean to ocean, and even those were pristine and teeming with life. But the human species thought otherwise. Now, thanks to humans, our Eden is shrinking. Soon it will be gone altogether. Human greed destroys everything. Not just our inheritance but their own, they destroy their own kind. "Do you know, Kaytek, that there are billionaires all over the Earth, while others are dying of starvation? Of thirst?"

Kaytek sat, spellbound. For once his thoughts didn't drift to treetops, to challenging crossings of streets filled with traffic, to sneaking into forbidden territories. He listened.

"And now, we are nearing the time when the Great Spirit will have to find a new planet, create a new reality, to fulfill the dreams we dream in Bardo. And when that happens, I pity the Humankind. What they did to our Earth, they will do unto themselves."

I have no idea why I lumbered Kaytek with my prophetic visions. Perhaps, that too was my job. Perhaps, the dreamers of Bardo will dream up a salvation. Yes, that must be it. Perhaps they'll dream of an Earth which we shall inherit in perpetuity. To live. To experience the joy of life.

I came closer to Kaytek and put my paw over his neck. He too moved closer, then snuggled into my fur. Soon our spirits merged. We became one. As one we travelled to Bardo. As one we shall start our dream of a New Kingdom. Then, I'd gently release him. I trust him to dream of New Earth and New Heaven. Of Paradise where nobody would eat a bad apple.

***

To Sleep or not to Sleep

"**Maytus?**"

One sleepy eye opened just a fraction, then quickly shut down again. His rich brown fur looked as real in this reality as in any other. His even darker point, the paws, the tail and the pointed ears gave him elegance seldom seen in a Cat. Even, what the humans call, a Siamese Cat. I suppose beauty is in the eye of the beholder.

"Maytus!" I had to insist, it's my job. Anyway, I wasn't really waking him up. "Yesterday was your second birthday, and it's time for your first lesson."

I had a soft spot for Maytus. It wasn't just that his colouring was near identical to mine, but, well, I felt like a mother to him. He invoked my maternal instincts.

Maytus was not really his name. In fact, the 's' should be softened into a sort of 'sh', a little like shushing someone in the middle of the night. His real name was Maytek, but the woman he recognized as his mother in every sense except the genetic, liked the diminutive. The real, human name would have been Matthew, but somehow it got distorted on the day he came to live with us. I really don't know how. I think it had something to do with his love of sailing, and, in Polish, Maytek means sailor, and... you've guessed it, his human mother was of Polish origin. The couple we stayed with, the Hoppers, Stephan and Bo was semi-retired, they owned a boat on Lake Champlain, and we all benefited from long weekends under sale. Stephan and Bo gave me a distinct impression that they considered themselves to be our parents. Genetic parents. Ha! Go figure! Together, Stephan and Bo, and Pimpah and Maytek and myself are a happy, a very happy family.

Maytek remained motionless. Sleeping or not, he was capable of remaining thus for hours. If you didn't know him as I do, you'd think he was lazy.

"You see, Maytek," I said stressing the word *see* to force his eyes open, "all cats have their purpose, as do all animals. You might not know this, but everything and everyone has a purpose to fulfill. That is why we were all created, often millions if not billions of years ago, and that is why we live.

If it weren't for the tip of his tail giving a slight wiggle, you would've sworn he was asleep.

"You probably also don't know," I continued unabashed, "that Bartholomew, the ancient who brought you here from Bardo, was ancient already in the days of

Noah. At the time of the Great Flood he occupied the body of Whiskers, the constant source of annoyance to Bart's son, the canine know-it-all, who liked to order us around."

I got his attention. Both eyes were now wide open, the ears pointed straight up, his attitude rapt if slightly disbelieving. I wondered if he was aware that he was still sleeping.

"You were pushed around by a dog?" There was undisguised horror in his voice.

I shrugged. "I said *liked* to push us around, not did."

That got his tail down. "Anyway, as for Bart—the Ancient Canine—he was just finishing his stint in physical world, being acclaimed an Enlightened Being, which, believe me, he was. Later, some three thousand years ago, humans borrowed the term from us and canines, and called it Bodhisattva, which you heard our hosts talking about. We'd all learned a lot from Bart. Though we don't often show it, Cats and Dogs learn a lot from each other."

"Cats learned from Dogs?" The disbelief in his voice was rising.

Maytek didn't seem to notice that while he was now floating some two feet above the ground, his physical body was still sleeping soundly on the grass below. Other than that he remained motionless, his large dark, almost black eyes that seemed to turn red at night, staring, unwinking, into mine. I took a deep breath. His attention was now fully aroused.

"If you remember the story of the Ark, Maytek. I was Purr in those days and, frankly, I purr better than most cats I know to this day." I was going to say *all* cats, but modesty is my second nature. I thought giving due where due was due rose above the pitfalls of pride.

"You were? Purr? So... you are sort of my great-

great-great-grand mother?"

I nodded and waited for the information to sink in. Instead, I heard Maytek doubling his effort to purr louder than ever before. Ah… children.

"And what's your job now, Grandma Maniusia?"

"My job is to teach dreams. Not to dream, only how to dream. And don't call me Grandma. I'm much too young," I said, licking my lustrous fur. It was as young as anybody's. Many a kitten would like to have my sheen.

"Ha! I dream! It's easy, I just close my eyes and bingo…"

"No, Maytek, not that sort of dream. I teach lucid dreaming."

Maytek ignored that. "And what happened to Pimpah?" She was to come back from the vet tomorrow.

I wondered where that came from. I hadn't mentioned Pimpah in this lesson. Not yet.

"Pimpah?" Dear, cute, sweet, wonderful Pimpah, "she gave meaning to Kaytek's, new embodiment."

"Ohhhh… that's why she could climb trees so well…"

Maytek already knew the story of Bartholomew taking Kaytek across the great divide. For us, Cats, different realities are easier to accept; easier then for humans, for instance. They are so anchored in material reality.

Yes… dear Pimpah. It had taken all of her courage to cross that street full of traffic. She's done it twice, trembling all over, and then decided that vertical exploration is more fun than horizontal. There are fewer automobiles running up and down trees. In fact, Pimpah made all the local trees her private domain. She didn't just climb them; she raced up to the very top, invariably forgetting that getting down is a lot harder. Her tiny talons were sharp-as-pins, alas, they were curved the wrong way.

Anyway, just about every time, before getting down, she made very sure that everyone within earshot saw her achievement. Did you know that she, too, dated back to Noah's time? It is quite common for families to reincarnate together, virtually as a group, though usually changing sexual orientation and actual relationships. I'm told humans do the same. After all, all sentient beings are immortal.

Without conscious awareness I conjured Pimpah running up a crabapple tree in our garden. Within seconds she was on the top.

Maytek continued to regard me with his penetrating, dark-brown eyes. Siamese have that ability. They can sit for hours, listening, sharing thoughts, philosophies. Not Maytek, of course, he's too young, but he's getting there.

Now, the tip of his tail began to make tiny swinging movement, left and right.

"She's not there, is she," he said, seemingly not taking eyes from my face.

I cleared my throat. It seems that the cat was out of the bag. Sorry, no pun intended. Maytek witnessed the first manifestation of lucid dreaming.

"Perhaps you only dreamt she was there," I said, trying to sound as innocent as I could.

"She still is," he said, still staring into my eyes. "Ouch!!!"

That came out when Maytek looked down and saw himself floating, by now, some four feet above the ground, which was the elevation I was at. He also drifted towards the tree, and, on falling down, he missed his physical body by a foot, saw it, jumped up from all fours, let out an horrified squeak and looked up at me. I was still up in the air.

Just for fun I made Pimpah come down, then run up the tree again. When she came down the second time, she tip-toed over and sat next to me. "You sure?"

Maytek was now licking his non-physical paws. Believe me. If you think you're hurt, you're hurt, only here non-permanently.

"Yes," he admitted grudgingly.

"So what do you think happened?"

"I'm dreaming." The answer was instant.

Step one, I thought. Now for the hard part.

"And just how do you know that?"

He looked at me in the way a 10 year old would when asked how much is 2 and 2.

"Sorry, a rhetoric question." I made Pimpah fade out of our picture. "Yes, my boy, you know that you know. And that makes it a lucid dream. How do you like it?"

For a moment he was lost.

"You mean this really is just a dream?"

"No, my friend. This is a dream in which you can decide on its out come. Picture a tree in front of you."

A tree materialized about a three feet in front of Maytek's nose. "Holly Bastet! How did that happen!"

I was about to say 'you dreamt it up,' but thought better of it. I waited to see what he'd do. Maytek got to his feet, made very sure he kept his physical body well behind him, and walked up to the tree. He smelled it on all sides, poked it with both front paws, then sat on his hunches and began staring at it like a Buddha in trance.

"Well?"

"It's a tree."

I smiled. "Why don't you climb it?"

"I don't climb trees," he said, his voice a little shaky. "Not like Pimpah."

"Nobody can climb trees like Pimpah, but do it the way you'd *like* to climb it."

The next moment I saw Maytek near the top of the crown, holding on to them in a passionate embrace. "H-h-how did I g-get here?" He almost stammered.

I let him stew for a little while. Then I asked him a simple question. "How do *you* think you got there?"

"Eh? I just saw myself on the top of the tree and…"

"…and there you were?"

"W-w-why yes…"

"Why don't you see yourself sitting next to me on this nice lawn."

"Just see myself… Great Bastet! What am I doing here?"

He was crouching on all fours, all knees bent, tail up, nose down, ears pointing to attention. I let him simmer for a minute or two. Soon his knees began to soften and he lowered himself to his belly. Then he licked his left paw. Then the other. Then, slowly, he turned his eyes towards me.

"So how do you like lucid dreaming, Maytus?"

"I can't get hurt?"

"Not unless you see yourself getting hurt."

"Mmmeeeoow!" It sounded more like the protracted meow I heard in a long time. It also sounded like a statement of disbelief tempered with unadulterated admiration. After all, he is a cat.

I thought that was enough for the first lesson. It's been a while since I taught Kaytek the same art, hoping to induce him to leave dangerous exploration to his dreams. Alas, as you know, I hadn't succeeded. Oh, he was a superb lucid dreamer, but then, later, he tried to do the same things in his physical body. Not advisable, or as they say, don't try this at home. Poor Kaytek.

Few Cats know this, but lucid dreams take place in the reality Bartholomew uses to take liberated cats across the Great Divide to Bardo. Sometime Cats linger longer here than they should. Old Bartholomew is too kind to stop them. They frolic together until the departing Cat would *normally* wake up in his physical body, and then Bartholomew puts them to sleep. Real sleep, not the shallow type we use on Earth.

In the meantime, Maytek was recovering from the shock of his first lesson. There was a great deal more to learn. Not just tree climbing, but manifesting reality, conjuring experiences, even visiting nearby planets. All that was yet to come.

"But it's so real, Grandma Maniusia, so very real..."

"I told you... make it aunt. Aunt Maniusia. Or Manka. It's as real as you care to make it. In this realm, you're a master of your reality. Then, you try to become a master in the physical world."

I left him to his musings.

Within weeks, he would be doing this completely on his own. He'd fall asleep and waken with eyes wide open. Once you accept the inner reality as real, it is quite easy. Even human could do it. If only they had someone to teach them.

In the meantime, Pimpah came back, sound and hale, but needing a little rest. That made her unusually stationary. This was just what Maytek was hoping for. A willing or otherwise, but fairly immobilized ear. The last I heard him telling Pimpah was about his trips to the Moon, Mars, Jupiter, Saturn, Neptune, Andromeda, three other galaxies. I stopped listening when he described to Pimpah, in great detail, the fun he had emerging on the other side of a gargantuan black hole. And this was after he circumnavigated the seven seas, single-handed, while she was at the vet.

"How about going next door, Maytek?" I asked. I was ignored with just a smidgen of contempt in his voice.

"Not now, Grandma. I'm busy."

Was he ever…

***

The Good Witch and the Warlock

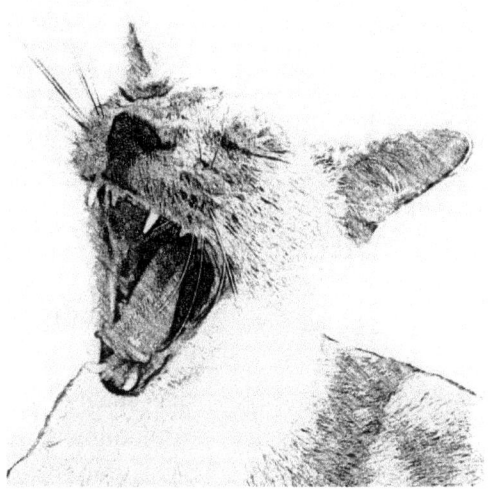

I'm sure you must have seen groups of Cats sitting in a rough circle, their ears all pointing towards the centre. Well, what you'd see would be only about one third of them. The other Cats remained invisible. They came from far and wide to take part in the meeting, forming a Witches' Circle. Here, in the altered reality, they positioned themselves at different levels. You wouldn't believe the variety. Fat Cats, nay... grossly obese Cats—which for some reason like to float at the highest level, scrawny Cats, Cats with torn ears. Even as I looked some of those ears began to grow to a perfect contour, as they should be in the altered reality. Bo, from our home, our Hopper family, calls the visible part of such get-togethers *Cats' Heavens*. Well, she's not far out. The rest of the Hopper family consists of Stephan, he's human, Maytek, Pimpah and, of course, myself.

About two months after Maytek has learned to enter the altered reality with hardly any help from me, came the next step. It coincided with the Autumn Equinox, the Solar Festival, September 21st.

I was ready.

I called The Coven—actually, it was also an Esbat, a witches' gathering for reasons other than to celebrate Festivals. I suppose, you could call me a High Priestess, but frankly, I was only doing my job. Today Maytek was to become a warlock. An unfortunate etymology is derived from Old English *wǣrloga*, meaning oath-breaker, or deceiver, but in fact, none of this true. Warlocks, like Witches, be then male or female, can be good and bad, like all cats. Anyway, Maytek was much too young to become a High Priest, and there was nothing in-between.

Actually, with the stories Maytek told Pimpah about his *very* imaginary exploits, the original meaning couldn't have been that far out.

For anyone who might be interested, since the days of Goddess Bastet in Ancient Egypt, the human withes' rites were loosely based on our liturgy. Not the other way round.

Anyway, I couldn't postpone the initiation any longer. If I had, they, the other witches, would take care of the initiation themselves, in a much more painful way. I've been an adept, a person highly skilled in Magick, since my last two embodiments. I could do it gently.

"Maytek," I called him with as gentle voice as I could muster.

"Yes, Grandma?"

"Aunt. Aunt Manka," I corrected him for the thousand's time. "Aunt Manka, or Maniusa."

"Yes, Auntie Maniusia?" His voice was sweet as trickle. He knew that when I spoke so very gently to him that always meant business.

"Today I am going to take you into the altered state, and I want you to swear to me on Goddess Bastet that you'll be on your best behaviour. Do I make myself clear?" My voice was so gentle I nearly scared myself.

"Yes-s-s, Aunt Maniusia. I will. Of course I will."

"You will what, Maytek?"

"I will be quiet as a Mouse."

Great Bastet! That would be the day. At any rate, there was little more I could do. We don't spank Cats.

Every time a new member of our inner circle becomes my acolyte I manifest my altar—my spiritual home—and call a meeting. Before the gathering came to order, I hung an amulet on Maytek's neck, just in case he needed extra protection. Then I cleansed him with a few drops of water. He didn't like that much, but, well, it is part of the ritual. A single "meouch" escaped his mouth as the drops landed on his face, but was quickly stifled when he noticed some witches hiding buckets of water, just in case I forgot to asperge him. There is no lack of humor in the Coven.

Then I manifested the Athame. It is a Witch's Sacred Knife. I admit, a bit scary.

"Not the *cohones*?" escaped Maytek's lips. His father was half-Spanish. Cats don't really have lips, but you know what I mean.

"Shhhhh!" I had to keep him quiet while the nearest

witches began to giggle. Athame is a knife consecrated for ritual use only. It only exists in the alternate reality, as in the lucid dreams. It can't be used for permanent physical damage, but is it one of the Four Witch's tools. I waved the knife twice in each of the four cardinal directions to disperse evil spirits.

Some distance away a bunch of banshees, as well as other little people—fairies, elves, gnomes and leprechauns—were making noise. I banished them to the four corners of the Earth. They were gone in a blink of an eye. All sorts of Little Folk appear around the Coven, trying to learn our secrets.

Our very, very sacred secrets.

When silence was restored, I read from the Book of Shadows. There is no one such book, and ours was tested by more then 500 generations of Witches skilled in Magick. This is not to be confused with magic, as in stage tricks. Magick is the knowledge of use of the powers of the mind, and the Universe, well beyond the conventional scientific laws. It belongs to arcane secrets of each individual Coven.

By now Maytek was hovering about three feet above the ground, his eyes sleepy, his body relaxed, his *cohones* intact. Only his tail seems to have developed some strange, jerky twitches. I never thought he was quite so nervous. All the same, I think he was beginning to trust me.

I nodded, and three of my assistants brought the censer, the chalice filled with charge, and the crystal wand, one of the Four Witch's Tools.

All was set.

"Maytek?"

"Yessss?" It sounded like a slightly nervous hiss.

"Pay attention."

His eyes opened wide. His tail stopped twitching.

Then, I went on to enumerate the characteristics of the five elements: Air, Fire, Water, Earth, and Spirit. All five were integral to any form of divination. We've learned this from Druits, who, even though human, were wise beyond their time. After each clause I read, the circle repeated in droning monotone:

So mote it be!

Meaning, so be it! Like amen, in some human religions.

Even as I read, I felt the Group Mind taking over. The other witches gathered in a Cone of Power. We were about to enter Maytek's deep mind. The part of his mind hidden from conscious probing.

The Chant began.

Now followed the part that I am not allowed to share with you, unless you are a witch yourself. It is the most sacred of rites, known only to the initiated. When it was over, I poured Libation from the Chalice in sacred offering.

The ceremony was over.

"Meow?" Maytus, the fearless warlock asked timidly.

I nodded. The next instant he was gone. I mean really gone. Gone from this reality. He must have jumped to his physical body. For a little while, he might well regard all this to have been just a dream. Some dream!

Maytek, the, oh… so recently baby Maytus, was now a fully-fledged warlock. Bastet knows, he didn't look like one. Quiet, seemingly complacent, purring his lungs out, sweet beyond words. Perhaps he did talk a little too much but, well, other than that he was a soft bundle of dark-brown fur. Cuddly.

For two days I saw him follow Pimpah, some two steps behind, wherever she went. She didn't seem to mind, as long as he didn't get too close. I rather suspect he was talking. Nonstop.

Every hour or so, he seemed to have become completely immobile. I knew what that meant. The thing was that one could leave one's body for literally seconds, and spend hours on the other side—in the alternate reality. He would emerge with his mouth open.

"Pimpah!" he would shout, and chase after her wherever she was. He needed to share every experience.

Now, with his new powers, he could enter the inner world at will, without any assistance. Once inside, his powers were virtually unlimited. It shouldn't matter much. In the inner world it is really hard to do any harm to anybody. Not even to yourself. However, none of us suspected that he'd attempt to use his powers in the physical world.

Alas, he was still very, very young.

Nevertheless, some of his exploits, strictly temporal, earthly, physical exploits, became the stuff of legends. After being grazed by an automobile, he crossed heavy traffic street, repeatedly, dodging charging automobiles, just to show his dexterity. He fought, and won, battles with a dog ten times his size, in defense of Pimpah. She'd never asked for help. In a blink of an eye she was already on the top of the tree.

Oh, yes! He was a knight in shining armour.

He also climbed the oak nearly to the top, just because Pimpah did it, (although, later, he had no idea how to get down). I caught him inches above the ground, whisked him to the Transition Land, and deposited him on the loan, where he woke up, later, in sound mind and body. Well, sound body, anyway.

As for his other exploits I saw them all in my crystal. I don't even dare repeat them. I was beginning to understand the old meaning of *wǣrloga*. Let us say, he was magnificently unpredictable.

Most of the time.

Maytus... my dear, dear acolyte. I also saw in my crystal that his life would be cut short prematurely. Out here, in dream-world, we don't see the future cast in stone, inexorable. What we see it the greatest probability; you know, like the humans do in quantum mechanics. But it's about ninety-nine percent likely.

I also saw Bo, tears streaming down her cheeks; Stephan, who chiseled his features into mask of granite... What is it that makes humans love us so much? We love them too, really, but we know that we don't really die— we just change realities. When will they ever learn?

When will they ever learn...

But just between you and me, Maytus knew. I cannot understand why he fought so hard to stay alive. For weeks. Long painful weeks.

Unless... unless he loved them just as much...?

What I did not see, at the time, was his last attempt to apply the warlock power outside its true domain. He drank poison, to show other, lesser cats that he can. Well, he couldn't. No one can break the laws of any reality with impunity. He suffered. All I can tell you is that at least for now, Bartholomew agreed to keep him in the Land of Transition, the land of lucid dreams, under his watchful eye. The last I heard, Maytek organized Cats on Ganymede, the seventh moon of Jupiter to form a Coven.

With himself as the High Priest, of course.

Do you have any idea how may Cats there are in the Solar System? They stopped counting after they reached 52 billion, and Ganymede, Jupiter's largest moon, is their capital city. I am told Maytek's thinking of expanding his influence to Callisto, Io and Europa.

High Priest!

Some boys just never learn.

***

Confirmation

(Or a story about not eating one's friends)

The stake was just a tad overdone. Suzan knew how I like it, but she chose to leave the grill for just a moment too long, to feed the cats. I hated playing second fiddle to our pets, but Suzan was gaga over them. I know both cats were my friends, but, well, lets face it, they could be a nuisance at times. When Suzan was away, my lap was as good as hers, but the moment she got back, I no longer existed. I, who daily cleaned their sandbox.

Friends?

For a moment I wondered if cats would be tasty, grilled or otherwise. For some reason, Piper, that's our female Siamese, had given me a dirty look. I shrugged. Obviously I'm seeing things. I reached for my Scotch and downed it in one gulp.

I refuse to be mesmerized by a cat. Most of all female cats. Women did it to me for years, but cats? Female cats? Perhaps I should eat them when Suzan wasn't looking.

There. There is that look again.

I looked the other way.

Stupid cat...

"Here you are, darling," Suzan joined me at the table. She didn't have a stake. Some kind of salad filled her plate to the brim. For a moment I had an image of a rabbit masticating all the green stuff.

For a while Suzan was trying to turn me into a vegetarian, let alone a vegan. Imagine, not eating honey because it was produced by bees. I think smothering them with honey, lightly basted, could make a tasty snack, though I wouldn't dare to tell Suzan that.

"Crunchy?" I mused aloud.

"What, darling?"

I gulped. "The chips are crunchy?" I asked.

"Just a little, but you like them that way, don't you, sweetheart?"

Rather chips than stake, I could have said, but thought better of it. Usually Suzan was an excellent cook. The overdone stake was an exception. And it wasn't her fault, I mused, giving Pipi, that's what we called Piper when we were alone, a dirty look.

She ignored me.

Pipi, not my wife.

"I spoke to Father O'Maley," Suzan changed the subject. "He said that on Saturday around twelve noon would be fine." Then she looked up at me. "The last mass is a eleven, the church should be almost empty by then. You won't be embarrassed."

O God... I whispered. *Thank heaven for little mercies. Thank God?*

For weeks, months more likely, Suzan, an ardent Catholic, was nagging me to undergo Confirmation, a rite that my early schooling hadn't offered. I thought it was only a Catholic rite, in fact a sacrament, but apparently other denominations indulged in it too. The Anglicans, which was the faith of my parents, but also Methodists, Lutherans, Later Day Saints, and who knew who else, liked to confirm, or seal, their Christianity created with Baptism.

"Do I need to take a bath first?" I asked innocently.

"I'll scrub you myself," Suzan offered.

Now that sounded a lot more fun than confirmation. I didn't mind other people indulging in their religious rights, I mean rites, but for me they all sounded like an escape from reality.

"And you'll wear a clean shirt and a suit," she added menacingly. Since my early retirement I tended to forsake the suits, ties and other paraphernalia of my professional life. Spending most of my time on the terrace, outside, slacks and a tee shirt were my favorite attire.

"Yes, dear," I added meekly, my mind wondering into the rites of bath scrubbing.

For some reason Pipi, and now Cuthbert, the male version of Pipi, regarded me with unusual, if not rare interest. Perhaps they forgot what I look like in a suit. No matter. I almost did myself.

"So it's tomorrow?" I asked at breakfast the next morning.

"At noon," Suzan confirmed. "Sharp!"

"I thought it was 'around'..." I still hoped to delay the inevitable.

This time both cats and Suzan regarded me as something a dog brought it. Perhaps I should have eaten both of them when Suzan wasn't looking.

"What did I say?" I asked. "I said I was going. After all, you did scrub me last night."

This elicited a surreptitious dirty look from Suzan, though it carried a smirk of amusement. The 'scrubbing' continued well into the night, both of us in our double bathtub.

So tomorrow I'd become a fully fledged Christian, let alone a Catholic. I wondered what name Suzan had picked for me. It made no difference, and one doesn't use it. It's just there for form's sake, I suppose. I forgot what the Jesuits taught me. After all, it was over fifty years ago and, on Einstein's advise, I worked hard to forget whatever I'd learned. I always thought that religion confined one's mind, rather than expanded it. Suzan disagreed.

As I finished my morning shower, a clean shirt, a suit I hadn't used for a couple of years and a blue tie, were laid out for me on the bed.

Suzan took her religion very seriously. I knew she suffered, a little, that I didn't, but I'm sure she prayed for me, daily. I had no idea why she wanted me to go to heaven, when her Savior said that "heaven is within you".

To each her own, I mused, each time such a subject came up.

"So... what's for breakfast?" I asked innocently.

"You're going to Holy Communion," she replied.

"But... I haven't been to confession in years!" I mumbled, my confidence draining from me.

"But... but..."

"You promised!" Suzan's voice was ice cold, filled with the antithesis of the indomitable Christian charity. After a few seconds she added more softly. "It's all taken care of. Father O'Maley is aware of your ah... shortcomings. He'll talk to you before the ceremony."

He did. In fact he was a man that was both kind and stern, smiling yet serious, a sort of father figure you only read about in books, but seldom meet. After chatting with him for a little while, he rose and invited me to join him in the church.

"I thought I had to, ah, do confession..."

Father O'Maley smile his paternal smile. "You did. What do you think we were doing the last ten minutes or so."

"That was confession?"

"John. This is the twenty-first century. You admitted a number of mistakes in your life, you're not proud of them, and you have no intention of repeating them. Your penance if what you are undergoing right now. I'm fully aware that you are doing it for your wife, and such evidence of love is more than I get in my confessional very often. Bless you, my son, and I'm sure God will do likewise."

I followed the Padre to the main nave. There were two other man and one woman waiting for us, seemingly waiting to be confirmed also.

Or, maybe they just arrived, I didn't know.

Suzan was in the first row of pews looking more beautiful than I've seen her for a long time. Something strange was going on in this church, but I couldn't put my finger on it. There was a silence that seemed to enter the deepest part of me. Silence and peace. A wondrous peace that I haven't experience for a long time. Perhaps since childhood?

The rite for the celebration of the Sacrament of Confirmation began almost at once. Usually, I've been told, it takes place during Mass, but seemingly Father O'Maley played by his own rules. Suzan had told me that he was delegated by the bishop to do so, to administer the Sacrament.

It seems that Father O'Maley was something special in more ways than one…

Then things got a bit hazy.

Do you reject Satan and all his works and al his empty promises?

The question reached me as though from a great distance.

"I do," I said, automatically.

Do you believe in God the Father almighty, creator of heaven and earth?

That same distant voice. I decided this was the wrong time to discus pros and cons of evolution, let alone astrophysics. And, after all, did we really know better?

"I do," I replied. After all, is God not a God by any other name?

Do you believe…

This went on for quite a while. I affirmed my faith without trying to analyze the philosophical connotations of the questions. After all, many, many years ago, I have been brainwashed by the Jesuits. The answers continued to come automatically.

Finally I heard:

Amen.

I wished I could have seen Suzan's face. She must have been happy. I was her personal achievement, her prodigal sun returning to the fold. Or was I? No matter, as long as she was happy.

Then there was the Laying on of Hands…

After many more words, some of them in Latin, and a number of 'amens' that continued to reach me from afar, the ceremony was over. Suzan came up to me, kissed me right there and then, at the main altar, slipped her arm under mine, and led me into the sunshine. I forgot to say thank you to Father O'Malley, but I'm sure he'll forgive me. After all, he had forgiven me everything else an hour or so ago. He was a good man, the old Father. Not as old as I was, but old enough to be called Father. At least his hair was almost a white as mine.

The next day, on Sunday, Suzan decided to serve a celebratory breakfast. A large orange juice, cornflakes, scrambled eggs, toast toasted to perfection, cheeses and a very good cherry comfiture. I was getting ready to be confirmed daily, if this was how confirmed husbands were treated. We took the second coffee on the settees, Suzan facing the window. I sipped my coffee slowly, extending the feast I've just been served.

And then it struck me that I forgot to ask Suzan what name she'd chosen for me. After all, it was all the same for me, but she must have had a reason for whatever she chose. I asked her.

"Didn't you hear the priest?"

I confessed to her that I seem to have been in some kind of semi-trance, which distracted my attention from the proceedings. I also told her that they said some words in Latin, and it's been many decades since I last uttered a Latin word.

"I sort of let the dead remain dead, as in dead language. The Jesuits overfed us at the time…"

"Francesco," she interrupted.

"Fran who?"

"'Cesco. Of Assisi," she completed.

"Francesco of Assisi? Frances? Isn't it a tad effeminate?"

"Not Frances. Francis," she corrected.

"Of Assi… wasn't he the fellow who loved animals?" I asked. "Birds, and things?" I added.

Suzan did not answer. She was staring intently a the window behind me.

"Suz an? What's up?" I looked behind me.

There, facing our French doors opening onto our garden, in a practically even semicircle sat four dogs and three cat. Next to each other, without any apparent animosity.

"Don't cats and dogs fight each other," I asked.

Suzan didn't answer. Slowly she got up and approached the window. The two branches of the apple tree nearest our terrace were literally covered with birds. For some reason the whole unlikely assembly of cats, dogs, and birds, all sat in utter silence. Then I saw Pipi and Cuthbert, also outside, walking towards our door with three more cats.

"What the hell is going on!?" I couldn't help exclaiming.

"I don't think you'll ever eat meat again," Suzan said very quietly, as though not to disrupt the silence of all the animals outside. The silence that reminded me of something. It wasn't just physical. Wasn't there such a silence in… church? Yesterday? And there was a sense of joy in Suzan's tone that I haven't heard for a long time.

And then she came to me and slid onto my lap.

"Thank you, Francesco. Thank you very much" she whispered.

I must have hallucinated, but looking over her shoulder, I couldn't have sworn that every dog and every cat and every bird was smiling.

I didn't know what to say, but I strongly suspected that she was right. That Francesco was up to his tricks again. And for some reason the idea filled me with great pleasure.

It was then that I realized that for Suzan, all animals were her friends. Not just cats and dogs, but pigs and cows, and horses, and birds like chicken…

Maybe even fish?

Oh, my, I thought. For Suzan the planet is replete with friends. She's surrounded by them. Like St. Francis? And, perhaps, she's right. One just simply doesn't eat one's friends. None of them. No matter how tasty.

Dear Suzan…

***

PIG
?

This time her chuckle turned into a prolonged giggle. Jane, my wife, was staring at a midsize piglet, which for all intents and purposes was staring right back a her.

"Winston was right," I commented trying to hide my own smile.

"I don't know any Winston," she replied, not taking her eyes of the pig."

"Churchill," I explained. "He said that dogs treat us as masters, cats and servants, and pigs as equals."

"John… It's staring back at me," Jane whispered, as though making sure that the pig wouldn't hear her.

We were on George's farm, taking a week off from the humdrum of city life. George and I went to school together. Then I went to study psychology and George returned to the farm to help out his aging father. The farm has been in the Wilson family for seven generations, hence, it seems, George was stuck with taking it over from his dad. Not that he did much farming. Three or four employees took care of most of the work. George's family seemed to be financially independent. Family money? Also, over the years, the farm became virtually self-sufficient.

Yet some traditions refuse to die, and, apparently, pigs were the farm's tradition. George's grandfather was the first to introduce pigs treated filtrate to irrigate crops.

Later, George's father began to use it also to generate his own power in biomass incineration plants. The resulting year-round heated pool was what attracted Jane and myself to the farm.

We remained friends since schooldays. Jane and I, as well as George.

Jane sat down on the grass, cross-legged in classical lotus position, and continued to stare at the piglet which remained perfectly still.

"Let's go?" I suggested.

She waved me down with her hand, otherwise remaining perfectly still.

"She's talking to me," Jane whispered.

I couldn't tell from my position if it was he or she, but I've long learned not to argue with Jane. Especially not after she waved me down.

"How can I?" Jane whispered. "No one would believe me, would they?"

I know this sounds ridiculous, but Jane was not talking to me, and there was no one else within earshot. Grateful for little mercies, I saw Jane untangle her legs from the tortuous yoga position, and smile sweetly at me, as though seeing me for the first time.

"Shall we go?" she asked, nodding towards the guesthouse. "It's almost lunchtime," she added.

We dined together in the main house, but Jane took care of breakfast and lunch. We didn't want to abuse George's hospitality. It was my job to assure that George's wine cellar was well stocked. It was. I had friends in the business.

Over coffee, I asked my wife what was going on between herself and the pig.

She smiled enigmatically. "I don't really know. I was asking questions and the answers appeared in my head. I have to sort all this out…" Her eyes got a bit hazy as she was answering me.

I knew I had to take it slowly. Jane had her 'poetic' moments in the past, but, well, never precipitated by a pig. I prodded gently.

"Sort what out…?"

This time she looked me straight in the eye.

"The pig was communicating with me by telepathy."

It took all my willpower not to smile, let alone laugh out-loud. I waited for her to continue.

"It all came at an incredible rate. Speed, I should say. It was as though she was using my brain as a quantum computer… Feeding me information on a dozen subjects at the same time."

I lost my smile. She sounded deadly serious.

"Pigs don't talk," I said very softly.

"Exactly. But there was no one else there," she looked at me long and hard, daring me to deny her. The silence stretched. "And the last time I communicated with you, you didn't use telepathy," she added superfluously.

It wasn't like her. She was never superfluous. Precise, rather then…

I sipped my coffee. I wondered if Jane began dipping her beak in my favorite Scotch, a 12-year-old malt I got in Scotland last year. I brought it with me on holidays, as George and family never touched anything stronger than wine.

"A brain on legs," Jane said after a prolonged pose. "It's coming to me in disjoined flashes. It all came in so fast…"

I kept quiet.

"The pigs said, I mean, you know what I mean, the pig told me that she was a brain on legs. This allowed for limited locomotion, and helped to remain incognito. By reducing the density of hair, the body manages to lose heat from the many trillions of neurons filling the whole trunk."

"Why?" I decided to play along.

"The brain is an electrochemical computer. It generates heat. Her brain it about fifteen times bigger than ours, and she uses about ninety percent of it…"

"As against us…"

"She said that ninety-six percent of our brain is used to administer our body. We are very physical species, which requires very specialized functions in our brain. Also our various systems are very complex. Just imagine keeping tabs on our cellular structure, repairing and or replacing defective cells. There are over 37 trillions of them alone, not to mention all the other systems. There is very little left in our brain for free-thinking… I wish I could tell you all this telepathically."

That, as it might be, I was still glad Jane wasn't a pig. Not even a telepathic pig.

"And... you heard all this from a pig?"

Jane had never manifested any interest in neurology.

"That's just it..." her voice lowered to a conspiratorial level. "They are not really pigs."

"You mean not all pigs are endowed with the gift of telepathy?" This time I couldn't help smiling.

"Although, from outside, there is no way to tell them apart," she mused aloud. "I mean the others are but she isn't..."

We finished our coffee in silence. After all, the subject was too absurd to peruse. I went to get my swimming trunks and hoped to clear my head with a few laps in George's pool. Minutes later, Jane decided to join me. We returned to the sitting room ready for our swim. The pool was accessible from either side, from the guest house and the main house. Convenient for both.

"She said she was an alien," Jane said as we entered to pool.

I preferred not ask 'who'. Jane seemed deeply preoccupied, as though in some sort of spell.

"They had all the animals at their disposal, and chose the pigs," she added, her toes testing the water. Apparently, we were still discussing the telepathic pig. "The most intelligent," she added.

"Including human?"

"So it seems." Jane smiled. "No darling. We have too small a cranium. With the neuronic needs they have our head would light up like a lighthouse. Or explode. Or at least our brain would boil over."

"Brain on legs, huh?" I mused. Jane nodded.

"Look at it this way. Ninety-six percent of your brain is busy administering your complex body. Also your body is much larger than necessary to evolve a functional AI. They, I mean... you know, the ah, pigs..."

She sounded both flustered and embarrassed as though what she was saying was secret yet obvious. After some deep breaths, she continued.

"They reduced their bodies to a trunk, four tiny legs for locomotion, and some external sensors for seeing, hearing, tasting, and receiving long-distance communications from their planet."

I scratched my prematurely balding pate.

"And she told you all that..."

"And a hell of a lot more. I'm still trying to convert it to thoughts that make some sense."

"You're kidding."

Jane looked at me. There was a plea and a command, simultaneously, shimmering in her eyes. I've never seen her looking like that. The next second she swirled and dove into the deep end of the pool.

And then, for some reason I heard Jane's thoughts in my head. At least, they must have been her thoughts...

You had chosen to develop your physical attributes. We chose the mental. Our body is our brain. All we had to do is to assure sufficient cooling system to get rid of the near infinite number of synapses firing all at once. We did this by maintaining a virtually hairless body. Rather like yours, only you keep covering yours up...

For a moment I was stunned. Was Jane communicating with me telepathically? And then I realized the voice said "*We*". "*We chose the mental*".

It isn't Jane. It's me.

I looked around. Jane was half way to completing her first lap. There was no one else present.

...but we can fly... by psychokinesis...

When pigs can fly... A famous adynaton. An obvious impossibility.

I also closed my eyes. This was too unnerving.

It took us quite a while to develop a receptive zoological structure in which we could spend any time in your environment. It was becoming quite taxing flying our ships in and out through your disgusting polluted atmosphere. They needed resurfacing after each landing.

An image of a flying saucer hovered briefly behind my closed eyelids.

And then I took a deep breath and dove into the pool. The warm water did little to dismiss my thoughts. I doubled my effort to catch up with Jane. She was waiting at the shallow end, a big smile on her full lips.

"You heard," she said. There was a girlish laughter in her voice as though she told me a great joke. "You heard," she repeated, this time laughing out loud.

I turned and continued swimming. I was sure that sooner or later I'd wake up. Because nothing would convince me that I wasn't dreaming. Even on my third lap.

We were sitting in the great hall. The house was so much more than a house. It was halfway to being a castle. The main hall that served as the dining room had a hammerbeam ceiling, with woodwork darkened with age, giving a sense of the passage of time. It must have been constructed during the gothic revival period, in early 19th century. All that was missing was an array of ladies in tight corsets, bonnets, bustles, and petticoats. And top hats, of course.

All we had were George and his wife, Clara, his elderly father, and two teenage children. The table could accommodate four times this number.

For some reason a vaguely uncomfortable silence stretched for a minute or two. Then George looked at me, his lips twisted in a wry grin.

"My dear, dear friend. Would you have believed me had I told you that I work for a pig?"

I was beginning doubt my own sanity. George was my friend for ages. Since school. He was a normal; as sane, as logical, as any man I've ever known.

"It all began with my great-grandfather..."

George sat back, half closed his eyes, as though recalling the past. Apparently, Sir Cuthbert Wickham, the third earl of Branham, has had a dream he couldn't shake off. It repeated itself about a dozen times, before he realized that he wasn't dreaming. What he was witnessing was real.

He had been told to raise pigs on his estate. At least two dozen, he was told. *"We'll take care of the rest,"* promised the voice in his head.

Indeed, his bank account received deposits from sourced unknown to him, though well documented. The rest was history.

He has been told that the human species is entering a dangerous period in its history. That within a few generations we were likely to develop technology that might upset the equilibrium of planets in the solar system. That, in turn, might adversely affect other systems, all relying on Universal balance.

...the nuclear power...

This was Jane, supplying the obvious.

"At any rate," the grandfather added, "the Galactic Confederation decided to keep an eye on us, until we grow up. Hence pigs... There are a few of them scattered around…"

"They are not pigs, of course," George interrupted his father's discourse. "They can control, telepathically, the brainwaves of dozens of men who hold the reins of our economy and the military. The whole world over. They do not infringe on our freewill, unless there is danger to the survival of humanity. Then a dozen options are available to them. Accidents, sicknesses, and if that doesn't work, then they tell the culprits the truth which makes them go insane, and they end up in a loony bin."

He took a sip of wine.

"Yes, in an institution for the mentally ill. After all, imagine a four-star general, or a Nobel Prize laureate in physics, telling his superiors that a pig told him to do this or that. The communication was of course subliminal, but it was accompanied with imagery that made it very real. After a little more persuasion, the big wigs decided to listen to their 'images' and behave."

I decided to play the role of a doubting Thomas.

"So, you are telling me that pigs are running the whole earth by not allowing us to cross the red line, right?"

No one spoke.

Silence stretched, interrupted only by heavy breathing. My own. The others seemed all relaxed.

Then the table, as long and heavy s it was, with all the chairs began to vibrate. Just slightly, like a G-string on a violin. Next it begun to rise up in the air. Not much. Just a foot or so.

Grandpa started laughing.

"To whom are you going to report this, son?"

It seemed that, at the appropriate moments, the pigs used psychokinetic means of persuasion. In addition to the floating table, images of pristine corridors of a lunatic asylum flashed before my eyes.

"It's OK, darling," Jane whispered. "No one would believe you anyway. You're not important enough."

So why tell me, I wondered.

We were back on the floor. Perhaps the table never moved. I wouldn't swear it did. I wouldn't swear to anything right then.

My head was rambling on a thousand ideas at the same time. We could stop feeding them. Or shoot them. Or…

Grandfather sighed.

"We all had such thoughts." Grandpa was either also telepathic or spoke from experience. Then he smiled. "They really do not hurt us, John. They help us. And if anyone tried to hurt them, they would fling this table at them faster than a speeding bullet. Psychokinesis is not limited to the velocity of light."

Then he fixed me with a surprisingly strong stare.

"And never forget, John. They are not pigs. Pig-like creatures are the biological computers they created to have influence on the rate of vibrations in our reality. That is all."

George got up, walked around the lengthy table, and put his hands on my shoulders.

"Welcome to the cognoscenti, John."

And then his voice softened.

"You are my best friend. You come here very often. Sooner or later you'd put two and two together and come up with a three-and-a-half. Which is exactly what happened to the whole family. And now it just binds us together."

At this the whole family rose to their feet and raised

their glasses.

"Welcome Jane and John."

The glasses clinked.

It was good to be among friend who didn't think that I was crazy. It was also good to know that the human race, in spite of its abysmal stupidity and homicidal tendencies, is likely to survive.

It was very good indeed.

****

A Word about the Author

Stan I.S. Law (aka **Stanislaw Kapuscinski**), architect, sculptor, and prolific writer, was educated in Poland and England. Since 1965 he has resided in Canada. His special interests cover a broad spectrum of arts, sciences and philosophy. His fiction and non-fiction attest to his particular passion for the scope and the development of Human Potential. He authored more than forty books, twenty of them novels.

Under his real name he published twelve non-fiction books sharing his vision of reality. He also composed two collections of poems in his original native tongue in which he satirizes his view of the world while paying homage to Bozena Happach's sculptures.

If you enjoyed his work, please be good enough to write a (brief) review wherever you bought the book and on Amazon. Your thoughts are important to us. Thank you.

Novels by Stan I.S. Law
http://stanlaw.ca

WALL—Love, Sex, and Immortality
[Aquarius Trilogy Book One]
PLUTO EFFECT
[Aquarius Trilogy Book Two]
OLYMPUS—Of Gods and Men
[Aquarius Trilogy Book Three]
AVATAR SYNDROME
[Avatar Trilogy Book One]
HEADLESS WORLD
[Avatar Trilogy Book Two]
AWAKENING—Event Horizon
[Avatar Trilogy Book Three]
YESHÛA—Missing Years of Jesus
PETER & PAUL—Intuitive Sequel to Yeshûa
MARVIN CLARK—In Search of Freedom
GIFT OF GAMMAN
ENIGMA OF THE SECOND COMING
MARVIN CLARK—In Search of Freedom
ONE JUST MAN [Winston Trilogy Book One]
ELOHIM [Winston Trilogy Book Two]
WINSTON'S KINGDOM [Winston Trilogy Book Three]
THE PRINCESS
GATE—Things my Mother told Me
ALEC [Alexander Trilogy Book One]
ALEXANDER [Alexander Trilogy Book Two]
SACHA—The Way Back [Alexander Trilogy Book Three]
NOW—BEING AND BECOMING
WINSTON TRILOGY Box Set
AQUARIUS TRILOGY Box Set

ALEXANDER TRILOGY Box Set
AVATAR TRILOGY Box Set

Short stories
THE JEWEL AND OTHER SHORT STORIES
Sci-Fi Series 1
Sci-Fi Series 2
Cats & Dogs Series

**Other Books by
Stanislaw Kapuscinski
(aka Stan I.S. Law)**
http://stanlaw.ca

VISUALIZATION—Creating your own Universe
KEY TO IMMORTALITY
[Commentary on the Gospel of Thomas]
BEYOND RELIGION I
BEYOND RELIGION II
BEYOND RELIGION III
[Each volume contains 52 Essays on Perception of Reality]
DICTIONARY OF BIBLICAL SYMBOLISM
VICIOUS CIRCLE (Volumes 1 to 6)
[In search of Secular Ethics]
DELUSIONS—Pragmatic Realism
CONCLUSIONS—Pragmatic Reality
PSALM 23 — Exegesis
ISAIAH —The Birth of Higher Consciousness
THE LORD'S PRAYER
SELF EGO VIRUS
DECALOGUE
THOUGHTS OF GOD

Published by **INHOUSEPRES**S Montreal, Canada

www.ingramcontent.com/pod-product-compliance
Lightning Source LLC
Chambersburg PA
CBHW071514040426
42444CB00008B/1637